T0059453

Thriving with Adult ADHD

Thriving
→ *with* ←
Adult ADHD

SKILLS TO STRENGTHEN EXECUTIVE FUNCTIONING

Phil Boissiere, MFT

ALTHEA
PRESS

Interior Designer: William Mack
Editor: Camille Hayes
Production Editor: Erum Khan

ISBN: Print 978-1-64152-272-4 | eBook 978-1-64152-273-1

Printed in Canada

To my ma'shaz amio—

*So many stars would have remained just out
of my reach, if not for your belief in me.*

Contents

Introduction: ADHD and You ix

1 What's Your Cognitive Style? 1

2 Sharpen Your Memory and Attention 15

3 Learn to Organize and Plan 44

4 Strengthen Your Mental Flexibility 66

5 Enhance Your Emotion Regulation 90

6 Improve Your Impulse Control 114

7 Live Your Best Life with ADHD 131

Resources 138

References 142

Index 145

Introduction: ADHD and You

Your Brain on ADHD

If you're reading this book, it's likely that you, or someone close to you, is dealing with adult Attention Deficit Hyperactivity Disorder (ADHD) and some of the many symptoms and complications it can cause. Adult ADHD can result in everything from impulsive decision-making to chronic lateness to irritability, and it takes a toll on the people who live with it. This book is designed to not only help you mitigate the impact your ADHD symptoms have on your life but also build the mental skills you need to actually overcome those symptoms over the long term.

Life is complicated, and we, as humans, have evolved many complex cognitive abilities that help us get through our everyday lives. From when we're babies, we learn to observe people and events in a variety of situations and respond in the most appropriate and effective manner. This includes simple verbal or behavioral responses to others' requests or statements, as well as more complex behaviors like planning, completing tasks, setting goals, and managing our emotions. In order to effectively navigate the myriad complexities we encounter, our brains develop what's called *executive functions* or *core skills*. These are some of the last cognitive functions to develop—not fully coming into their own until we're in our 20s—and they're key to smooth functioning in adult life. These important skills are the core of what adults with ADHD struggle with in their daily lives.

I'm a therapist who has been working with adults with ADHD for a decade. Those of us in the clinical and scientific communities are not 100 percent clear on the exact underlying causes of ADHD, but we do know with certainty that the prefrontal cortex (the front of the brain) is a major player. This part of the brain is where the ever-important executive functions (core mental skills) are housed. Think of it as the big corner office where the CEO makes all the important decisions.

This book will help you develop the skills you need to strengthen your mental CEO with a series of powerful exercises, tools, and proven strategies for bolstering your memory, organizational skills, and even your stress management. Whether you will use the skills to get to meetings on time, plan and complete projects, navigate intense emotions, or develop new ways of thinking about yourself and the people and events around you, having a good grasp of them will get— and keep—you on track and moving toward the kind of life you want.

Workouts for Your Mental Skills

Picture for a moment that CEO in the big corner office. How did she get there? Was it through endless procrastination, distraction, and emotional overwhelm? Not likely. She probably got there because her prefrontal cortex—the command center of the brain—is dialed in and making things happen. The cluster of skills related to executive functioning—things like memorizing, organizing, and planning—are, no doubt, central to her success. To get your skills into CEO-level shape, you'll need to do some workouts to build your strength. Think of these strategies as your new cognitive workout routine.

Advanced executive functioning skills are much more than learning how to make a to-do list or organize your calendar. The skills everyone needs in order to excel in work and life must allow us to navigate all aspects of any situation, no matter how complex. Let's take a look at a real-life example to illustrate where and how these skills come into play. Imagine this: Your phone rings, and it's an important client demanding your attention. They are complaining about something big, and they require clear and concise responses from you. After the call, you must put together a plan to meet your client's needs, and you will also have to stick to that plan and get it done. Because your client is upset, there won't be time to surf the web, dabble in online shopping, or disappear into the abyss of social media—you have to get the job done ASAP. This isn't an uncommon scenario in the lives of most professionals; but if you have adult ADHD, you might be getting nervous just reading this example, because you already see the pitfalls it contains for you, including planning, maintaining focus, and thinking clearly under pressure. The symptoms of ADHD present a real barrier to developing and using precisely those types of skills.

Let's take a closer look at exactly what the relevant skills are in the "unhappy client" scenario. In a situation like this, you will probably feel a whole range of emotions, such as anger, embarrassment, defensiveness, or fear. To effectively handle the situation, you need to control those emotions so you can respond in a calm, polite, and nondefensive way. You also need to keep your emotions under control in order to think clearly—after all, a stressed-out mind is a scattered mind. And you need to respond to the client in a clear way that is not impulsive. Shouting, saying yes to a big demand without thinking, or breaking down in tears is not the best response.

Finally, you need to execute your plan in a timely manner and leave the client feeling that his needs have been addressed.

That's a lot of complex skills to bring to bear on a single situation. The good news is, this book teaches you how to build all of them. Among other vital skills, you'll learn techniques for making manageable plans and meeting deadlines without the stress and pressure of procrastination. Emotion regulation exercises are provided so you can learn to stay calm even in tough situations. And I'll walk you through all kinds of other cognitive "workouts" that will leave your skills and coping strategies much stronger than when you started. In other words, at the end of this book you will have a big toolbox of skills that will allow you to get organized, hone your focus, keep your emotions in check, meet deadlines, and reach even your most ambitious self-improvement goals. That's right—these same techniques are as helpful at home as they are at the office. You may need them to tackle home improvement projects and parent-teacher conferences, rather than board meetings and sales calls, but either way, strong mental skills will get you where you want to go faster and more efficiently.

Do You Have ADHD?

This assessment tool will help you determine which of the most common ADHD symptoms are causing the biggest problems in your day-to-day life. Please keep in mind that a short checklist like this is not sufficient to officially diagnose ADHD. Only an assessment conducted by a trained health provider can do that—contrary to what the Internet might say. However, this checklist will show you how much you're struggling and which specific areas need the most attention.

The following list of symptoms is adapted from the brief ADHD screening tool used by the World Health Organization:

- You often struggle to finish projects.
- You have difficulty getting organized.
- You have problems remembering appointments.
- You avoid or delay getting started on tasks.
- You tend to feel overly active and compelled to do things.
- You make careless mistakes.
- You have a hard time keeping focused on boring or repetitive tasks.
- You regularly misplace or lose things.
- You get distracted by things going on around you.
- You feel restless or fidgety.
- You often talk too much or blurt things out.
- You struggle to wait your turn.
- You tend to interrupt others when they are busy.

If you found yourself saying, "Yes, that's me," or "How did you get inside my head?" or just plain broke down in tears reading this list because the struggle looked so familiar, you may want to talk to your health provider about taking a deeper look into the possibility that you might have ADHD.

How to Use This Book

There are a couple of ways to use this book. You may already be working to manage ADHD or related issues and just want to home in on specific skills for memory or organization, for example. If that's the case for you, just skip right to the parts of the book that resonate with you. However, most people reading this book will want to follow the book in order, completing all the exercises and building a strong arsenal of skills to help them excel in any challenging situation. Don't worry; there will be no annoying coach barking orders at you or parent making shame-inducing comments—this book is just you and me side-by-side, partnering to unlock your potential and make life much more manageable. I really want you to hear that: *I am on your team.* Leave at the door any shame and self-doubt that life with ADHD has handed you.

If you want to maximize the results you'll get from the great practical information in this book, start thinking about this process as a way to develop real and sustainable change in all the important areas of your life. For example, the very same skills that you'll learn for managing impulsive behavior and intense emotions will help you respond calmly to your boss, your spouse, your kids, your annoying neighbor, and even the family dog. The skills for improving focus and task completion will help you rock your big project at work, efficiently shop for groceries, finish that college degree, or even complete your online dating profile. What I'm saying to you is that your executive functions and their associated skills are critical to succeeding in all aspects of your life—period. And you are holding in your hands a powerful tool to help you learn those skills.

I recommend starting your journey through this material by obtaining a small pocket-size notebook. You will use this notebook to complete exercises as we go along. So go get your notebook, and I'll be waiting for you in chapter 1.

1 What's Your Cognitive Style?

The Core Skills

In order to organize and make sense of the different types of executive functions and their associated skills, I have organized them into clusters that we'll call the *core skills*. But before we go into detail on those, let's take a big-picture look at the role these skills, as a group, play in our lives. They are behind most of the heavy lifting your brain does on any given day. They are certainly critical to navigating life successfully. Your ability to pay attention, decide on a plan, think critically, manage intense emotions, and keep impulsive behaviors in check relies almost exclusively on these mental skills. Remember in the introduction, when I explained that executive functions and core skills reside in the prefrontal cortex (PFC)? This is the large part of the brain located right behind our forehead and eyes. It's also the part of the human brain that sets us apart neurologically from other mammals.

When we're babies, the PFC is barely formed. Babies don't plan, regulate emotions, or care about impulsivity—they do what they want, when they want, and how they want. Pulling on Grandma's earring looks fun. *Yank!* Time for a bathroom break with no diaper on? Great! The couch looks like a perfect place to go potty. Feeling hungry? Shove Dad's laptop to the ground and reach for your bottle. Feeling cranky? Just scream until you're exhausted. Then take a nap and start the whole process again when you wake up. The lack of a fully developed PFC is why babies need to be monitored so closely—they can't be trusted to manage themselves, because they don't yet have the cognitive skills to do so.

Fortunately, the PFC eventually does develop—although unfortunately, it is not fully formed, on average, until we're about 25 years old! This is why teenagers make such crazy, impulsive choices. The emotional center of their brain is in full bloom, but the brakes and logic centers are just beginning to bud. By our mid-20s, most of us have a fully functioning PFC—although we're not all equally adept at using its advanced functions. I'm sure my wife and kids wonder if my PFC even exists at times, but I'll save those stories for my memoir.

Even adults with normally developed executive functions can struggle to make full use of them, but when you have ADHD, your challenge is even greater. That's because ADHD wreaks havoc on these functions to varying degrees. To run smoothly, they require the availability of a large amount of specific neurotransmitters in the brain, mainly dopamine and norepinephrine. These are the main chemicals that ADHD medications target, because they are often not being produced or efficiently used in people with ADHD. Dopamine is critical for achieving goals and the feeling of reward or sense of accomplishment. Norepinephrine helps to quiet down all the noise in the environment and in our minds. Remember, often the most distracting things you encounter are your own thoughts and feelings. When dopamine and norepinephrine are working together, it's easier to know what to focus on and what tasks need to be carried out. If you have ADHD, your brain's inability to access these neurotransmitters in adequate amounts is part of what leads to distractibility and an inability to focus, which are hallmarks of the condition.

As important as dopamine and norepinephrine are, they don't account for all aspects of your core skills. As with so many things, individual variability accounts for a lot. No two people are the same, period. Some people are good at planning, some are good at focusing, and some seem good at everything. It's no different for people with ADHD. ADHD can be downright debilitating for some people and very mild for others. The first step in understanding how to manage your own symptoms is to determine what your individual strengths and challenges are. Even when people have similar severity in symptoms, they can still have different strengths and weaknesses in their core skill set. Regardless of your individual profile, one thing is true across the board: ADHD can be *very* frustrating. It damages careers, disrupts relationships, makes parenting harder, and can make people feel ashamed. The many challenges this condition presents can truly bring people to tears.

The good news is that ADHD can be managed—and managed pretty darn well, at that. This chapter will help you determine which areas you're struggling with the most and which ones aren't so bad. Essentially, you'll develop a loose framework to understand your particular cognitive style. The way in which people think and act varies so much that you may have a hard time pinning down precisely which skills are causing you problems. You might be great at analytical thinking. You might be able to use your analytical thinking to come up with incredibly insightful and valuable solutions. Yet, your inability to focus and plan may keep your incredible ideas trapped in your head. Someone else might thrive under intense and adrenaline-fueled crisis situations but not be able to sustain enough focus to make coffee in the morning.

These gaps between mental and demonstrated skills can make people feel terrible. "If I can do x, then why can't I do y? What is wrong with me?!" It's important to point out here that there is no link between intelligence and ADHD. Having ADHD doesn't make you "dumb" or less capable; it means that the way your brain functions makes certain tasks more challenging than they are for others who don't have those symptoms. Knowing even a little bit about your personal style of thinking is empowering. You can take stock of your stronger areas and brush up on the things that are challenging. Heck, you may even be able to leave some weaker areas behind and strengthen others to offset the difference.

Finding Your Style

Let's look more closely at the core areas of executive functions and see what you may want to focus on most. Below, you will find a brief overview of each area. After each overview, you'll answer 10 questions. Please write your answers to each quiz in your notebook for reference later. Remember, these brief assessments are not a clinical diagnostic tool. Rather, they're a quick way to gain insight into how you're doing in each of the core clusters of cognitive skills.

Quiz instructions: Get out your notebook and a pen. For each question, you will write down 0, 1, or 2 depending on your personal experience. The answers should be what you believe about yourself, not what other people think about you.

0 – No or never
1 – Sometimes
2 – Yes or often

If you score a total of below 10 on a particular area, then you're basically doing fine with those skills and that's not a very important area on which to focus your efforts. However, if you answered any individual questions in that area with a 2, it may be important to address those subareas.

If you score a total of 10 or above on any of the core areas, that's an area in which you will need to make an effort to improve your skills. Note: If you score above 15 in an area, you will need to try a little harder to improve that area.

ATTENTION AND FOCUS

This section assesses your ability to focus attention on demand and on the appropriate things. You will often find yourself in situations where there are competing distractions, and the ability to filter out the "noise" is critical to maintaining focus. Also, you may have to do tasks that are downright boring, but you still need to harness adequate focus and attention to complete or engage in the task. Issues related to attention and focus are the most common set of struggles for adults with ADHD.

ATTENTION AND FOCUS ASSESSMENT QUIZ

1. I tend to be easily distracted when activities are happening around me.
2. I struggle to finish work or school tasks.
3. My attention wanders easily when I am working or studying.
4. I get distracted and lose focus when I hear noises or see things in my environment.
5. Novelty is nearly impossible for me to ignore.
6. It is hard for me to listen to what people say to me.
7. I can usually only focus when something is very interesting.
8. I get lost in thought or daydreams while reading or doing similar tasks.
9. I tend to focus on the wrong things.
10. People often ask me if I am listening or paying attention to them.

ORGANIZING AND PLANNING

This section assesses your ability to be organized in your daily life, as well as the ability to plan ahead. It also takes a look at your ability to initiate tasks and commit things to memory. Being organized is very important for keeping life manageable and less stressful. A disorganized physical environment can lead to increased distractions. Also, when you haven't planned out your projects or activities, it's easy to procrastinate and get distracted, which can lead to overwhelm.

ORGANIZING AND PLANNING ASSESSMENT QUIZ

1. My estimate of how long it takes to do a task or go somewhere is often wrong.
2. Organizing tasks and activities is very difficult.
3. I often lose important items I need for work or other tasks (lists, notebooks, pens, tools, and so on).
4. I never plan ahead.
5. I am rarely organized.
6. Forgetfulness is a daily or almost daily occurrence for me.
7. Without a clear deadline, I will never get a task done.
8. Starting work, school, or home tasks is hard for me.
9. I avoid planning the steps necessary to complete a project.
10. My work or home space is cluttered and can feel overwhelming.

MENTAL FLEXIBILITY

This section assesses your ability to exercise flexibility in thought, which ultimately drives behavioral patterns. Mental flexibility, also referred to as cognitive flexibility, is critical to having multiple options in any given situation. This skill is also very important in your ability to shift your perspective and develop new beliefs.

MENTAL FLEXIBILITY ASSESSMENT QUIZ

1. I have trouble letting go of the mistakes I made in the past.
2. I struggle to keep track of several things at once in my mind.
3. It's hard for me to recognize alternate options in most situations.
4. I lack self-confidence, even in tasks I am good at.
5. I'm not able to reflect on my thoughts easily.
6. I don't like work or school tasks where I need to think a lot.
7. Changing my opinions or beliefs is very hard for me.
8. I have a hard time seeing another person's perspective.
9. I decide on outcomes without any proof and then stick by my conclusions.
10. Brainstorming new ideas or solutions is hard for me.

EMOTION REGULATION

This section assesses your ability to regulate, or control, your emotions and responses to emotions. Emotions have a direct effect on everything we do. An emotion that's too intense hinders performance, colors perceptions, and can lead to procrastination, distraction, and strained relationships.

EMOTION REGULATION ASSESSMENT QUIZ

1. I get irritated very easily.
2. Mistakes make me very upset at myself.
3. I am impatient.
4. I am easily frustrated by other people.
5. I am easily angered and have a short fuse.
6. When I don't get my way, I get visibly upset.
7. My mood is not consistent and changes easily.
8. I get set off by many things.
9. Difficult emotions (anger, sadness, frustration, and so on) are hard to let go of.
10. I tend to shout or storm out of the room.

IMPULSE CONTROL

This section assesses whether you struggle with impulsive behaviors, decisions, and choices. The ability to behave appropriately is fundamental to succeeding in any environment where you interact with other people. It is also critical to making choices that are good for you and help, not hurt, your progress in life.

IMPULSE CONTROL ASSESSMENT QUIZ

1. I interrupt people regularly when they are busy with a task.
2. When asked a question, I tend to answer before the person finishes asking the question.
3. I blurt things out with very little control.
4. I am an "adrenaline junkie."
5. I often talk way more than others around me do.
6. Statements come out of my mouth before I have given them much thought.
7. I can't stay seated for very long.
8. I switch tasks or activities abruptly midstream.
9. I wish I could take back many things I have said.
10. I annoy other people without meaning to.

Strengthening Your Cognitive Skills

So, what were the results of this brief assessment? Were you surprised at the areas in which you tend to struggle? Were there areas where you're doing better than you thought? I want you to make sure that you don't focus just on your difficult areas. It's important to note the areas where your functioning is stronger, because your cognitive strengths will be your best ally in managing your ADHD symptoms. You may want to rank the areas from the highest score to the lowest. This will allow you to quickly see which areas need the most effort to improve. It will also allow you to develop a broad profile of your cognitive style. No two people are the same. For example, you may really struggle with regulating emotions, organizing and planning, and controlling impulses. But another person's biggest struggles might be with attention and focus, mental flexibility, and emotion regulation. You need to know about your specific areas so you can prioritize the skill-building techniques introduced in the following chapters.

Please keep in mind that ADHD is not a temporary condition—the strategies you'll be learning are meant to last a lifetime. When people are living well with ADHD, it means they've become good at managing it and leveraging their particular cognitive styles to help them thrive. I will discuss this more in the following sections.

YOUR PLASTIC BRAIN

No, your brain is not actually made of plastic because you have ADHD. It is made up of the same incredible assortment of cells, nerves, and tissues that are in all mammal brains and nervous systems. When we refer to something as having *plasticity*, we mean it is flexible and can be changed. For decades, scientists believed that your brain developed during childhood and then stopped—that it was locked in place and couldn't change. Fortunately, brain imaging studies and other research breakthroughs have shown us that the brain is capable of incredible change throughout the lifespan (see, for example, Fuchs and Flügge 2014). Granted, it's harder for someone to change their brain at 75 than it is at 35, but it's not impossible. Neuroplasticity does not mean the brain changes shape in some dramatic way. The change is at the level of nerve connections, meaning that neuroplasticity allows you to change the way your brain is wired. The proven exercises in this book will help you do that.

GETTING IN SHAPE FOR ADHD

When someone lifts weights, the muscle fibers are torn and rebuilt bigger and stronger. Learning a new workout routine or exercise in the gym can feel awkward and take a lot of effort at first, but it quickly becomes automatic and much less difficult. The same is true for the exercises in this book. Your initial efforts should yield results and get you feeling better pretty quickly. As you continue to use them, over time you will get stronger and stronger. I bet you will look back a year from now and find that many of your current biggest struggles seem small. I also bet that using these exercises and skills will be second nature, like taking a shower or brushing your teeth.

Think of ADHD as a marathon you'll be running. The key thing that sets marathons apart is that they're long. Managing your ADHD symptoms is a long-term proposition, too. Like marathon training, you'll have good days and bad days, fast days and slow days, or days when you are injured and need to recover. Lifetime management of ADHD is a journey with many twists and turns. You will work at it daily, and you will improve. You will have productive and focused days, you will have days where nothing seems to click, and you will have days when you accomplish more than you ever thought possible. If you are in this for the long haul, to live a better life by putting in the effort and reaping the rewards, you are in the right place.

Let's look at how behavior and habits can actually change for people with ADHD. One of the most common complaints I hear in my office is, "I start doing something new to manage my ADHD, but I always fall off. I just can't keep anything going!" I think anyone reading this book can empathize with that perspective. Just think about New Year's resolutions. Come January 1, every athletic club or gym fills up with people—so many new members in their fancy sneakers hitting the treadmill or spin class. Come February 1, there's almost no one in the gym. What happened? Did all those people meet their goals and move on? Absolutely not. They fell off the exercise wagon right into a bag of chips while binge-watching their favorite shows. Will this happen to you as you set out to manage ADHD? Sure, it will. But what will set you apart is the wealth of skills you will have developed—not just skills for improving, but skills to get you back on track quickly.

READY TO START?

The messages you tell yourself are going to make a big difference. Most of the time, when people say things to me like, "I've tried a to-do list or a timer, and it didn't work," they also tend to say something else once I dig a little. They will tell me that they hit themselves over the head with negative self-talk after as little as one day of not using a skill. "See, Johnny? You can't do anything right. You'll never change." But that's just plain wrong. I've watched hundreds of people thrive in the face of nearly crippling ADHD. It's time to leave that way of thinking behind. It's time to leap on the horse and ride.

You are reading this book and embarking on this journey of improvement because you know you're capable of more—because you *want* more. You want to be more for the people in your life that you care about. You want to be more for yourself.

I want to quickly point out a potential pitfall to avoid. Many people will be tempted to dive into this book and crank though it in a week. That's a mistake. It will undoubtedly feel good to complete it and get all these incredible tools under your belt, but if you do it that fast, they won't stick. The skills and exercises in this book take practice and time to become "go-to" skills. You will likely benefit most if you do a minimum of 20 to 30 minutes of work on it a day. I recommend that you decide, with intention, when you will be working through this book. Once you decide, put it on your calendar. Remember that you are doing this because you want to. You want real change. You want to break the chains of adult ADHD and fly high.

Takeaways

- There are core mental skills that help you navigate life.
- Your personal cognitive profile will, in part, determine your particular strengths and challenges with ADHD.
- Your brain is "plastic" and capable of change.
- Managing ADHD is a lifelong practice with lifelong positive outcomes.
- Exercising your executive functions to develop skills is just like building your physical muscles.
- You are on this journey because you know you deserve better and are capable of much more.

2 Sharpen Your Memory and Attention

Overview

Attention and memory are inextricably linked. The ability to pay adequate attention in any given moment is critical to creating memories. In fact, most of what we call "forgetting" is the result of the memory not being fully formed in the first place. We never had a firm hold on the memory, so it slips through our grasp. When a memory is created, it follows a path that starts with attention or awareness, at which point the information enters into the working memory, then the short-term memory, and then, finally, the long-term memory for extended storage.

Given how important attention and focus are to creating memories, it makes perfect sense that adults with ADHD tend to have considerable trouble with memory. Forgetting what you're doing, what you had for lunch yesterday, or whether you completed a project is a painful daily reality for many. When you forget things, it tends to cause frustration for you and the people who are counting on you. Forgetting tasks, important information, or people's names often triggers shame, as well as increased anxiety and self-doubt when you are exposed for forgetting something. This can lead to a nasty cycle of more problems with memory, more anxiety, and more shame. You deserve better, and you're capable of getting it.

In this chapter, you'll learn how to get better at staying on track, boosting your memory, and harnessing your ability to focus at critical times. The types of struggles related to memory for people with ADHD are so common that they are almost cliché. Heck, if they weren't so frustrating and painful, they might make great T-shirts or bumper stickers. Unfortunately, ADHD is not a cute slogan on a T-shirt, and it has very real impacts on success. The skills laid out in the following pages will help you retain and follow instructions, manage distractions, reduce those painful moments of "Why did I come in here? What am I doing? What was I about to say?" and much more.

Depending on your work or lifestyle, you may need some of these skills more than others. People who work on long, multi-part projects will benefit greatly from sustaining focus and breaking projects into manageable parts that can be accomplished using bursts of focus. People who operate in chaotic environments like a home or school with multiple children are going to benefit from improving their working memory. No matter which area of your life focus and memory negatively affect, you will gain skills to rise to the challenge. Let's get going.

Strengthening Working Memory

When you think about memory in general, you likely picture the people, places, things, facts, experiences, and other knowledge you have collected over a lifetime. A memory for you might be the first phone number you ever memorized or a visual image of your elementary school. It's correct that those are memories, but they are not part of your *working memory* (WM), which is what we're focused on here. Your first day of school, your first kiss, the time your cat got stuck in a tree, and learning to drive are important life events, but not the kind of memories that lead to struggles in daily life. If you forgot any of those things, it might be sad, but it wouldn't get in the way of effectively doing a task. For that, you need working memory. Your WM is about remembering what you are doing in the moment and retaining all the information you need to execute the task at hand. In fact, your WM is exactly what's being used while you're reading this page. The paragraph or sentence you are on and the topic of this chapter are being held in your WM.

Walking into another room and having no clue why you went in there, forgetting where you just put your pen, and even putting the cereal in the refrigerator and the milk in the pantry are all examples of breakdowns in WM. Struggles like these are becoming more common for people, with or without ADHD. Overuse of smartphones and tablets has led to nearly constant task switching, which taxes our WM. Every time you jump from one task to the next, it creates a strain on your WM. I've never worked with a client who has not struggled with task switching—I struggle with it, too. To focus on writing this book, I made sure my phone was turned off, my e-mail was closed, and notifications of all types were silenced.

The WM is just one of the many important functions that the brain carries out every minute of every day. Therefore, strengthening WM must include the health and functioning of the whole brain. For example, I often give workshops on stress and performance. Most people in the course are surprised to find out that the most common sign of being too stressed is forgetfulness. Stress causes the release of hormones that have a direct negative impact on our ability to make and retrieve memories. The two most consistent ways to improve mental functioning and, therefore, memory are to sleep and to exercise. We know that exercise is very important for improving ADHD symptoms, and it turns out it's good for memory also. The exact reasons for this are not totally clear, but we do know that exercise reduces stress. ADHD causes considerable stress for most people, so exercise may just kill two birds with one stone. Sleep also helps regulate stress and allows the brain and body to repair. If someone is not getting adequate sleep, they will have trouble with focus and memory. It's easy to be jaded about sleep and exercise, because they are things you probably already know you need more of. So, let's take a look at some concrete tips for strengthening your working memory.

(tip) Keep your brain sharp with movement and exercise. On a daily basis, make sure to get even a small amount of exercise. It's best to do about 30 minutes of an activity that elevates the heart rate. However, 10 minutes of stretching or a short walk around the neighborhood also have positive benefits.

(tip) Protect your sleep. Decide on target sleep and wake times. Getting eight hours of sleep will never happen without a plan. Many people find going to sleep at 10:00 p.m. and waking up at 6:00 a.m. to be manageable. Decide on a time frame for yourself, and let the appropriate people know that you are going to follow it.

(tip) Label or name a current task before doing something else. If you need to switch to another task or temporarily interrupt what you're doing, simply state to yourself what you are working on and what you need to return to; for example, "I'm gathering my expenses for my accountant. I need to pick back up with June 2017 expenses."

(tip) Use positive self-talk. When you have forgotten what you are doing, be kind to yourself. Kicking yourself with negative self-talk about messing up will make it worse. Instead, say things to yourself like, "It will come to me. No big deal."

CREATE A NARRATIVE

It can be extremely helpful to create a narrative or story about the task or activity you are about to do. It will reduce the probability that you will forget what you were doing or get distracted.

1 Identify the task you need to do. Make sure to choose something that isn't too complicated. Examples of tasks that work well for this exercise are hanging a painting, cleaning out a closet, compiling documents for a client, and so on.

2 Tell yourself a story with a beginning, middle, and end that includes all the steps of the task. If it helps, get out your notebook and write it down.

3 Do the task!

EXAMPLE *Araceli needed to hang two paintings in her living room, so she created this narrative of the necessary tasks: "First, I'm going to gather my hammer, nails, and hooks. Then I'm going to walk out to the garage, get the painting of the horse and the one of the cat, and bring them into the living room. Next, I'll decide where to hang each painting in the room. I will then nail the hooks into the wall. Finally, I will hang the paintings and sit down on the couch and observe my accomplishment."*

Professional athletes practice game plays, soldiers practice military missions, astronauts practice simulated space flight—and you can benefit from simulated practice, too!

1 Do steps 1 and 2 from the previous exercise, but this time with a new task.

2 Ask a friend or family member to interrupt you with a question while you are doing your task (step 3 from the previous exercise). When they interrupt you, tell them you are happy to answer them or help them once you finish doing your task. After you say that to them, repeat to yourself either the part of the task you are doing or the part of the task you are on your way to do.

EXAMPLE *Araceli is walking to the garage to get the two paintings she wants to hang. Her spouse calls to her from the home office as she walks by, "Araceli, what color of paint do we want in the hallway?" Araceli pauses and says, "Good question, Jacob. I've got some ideas and will share them with you once I finish this task." She then says to herself (out loud or in her mind), "I'm on my way to get the painting of the horse and the painting of the cat from the garage."*

Improving Overall Memory

Overall memory is what most people think of when memory is mentioned. Overall memory is our stored knowledge of details, life events, names of people, and so on. To get your brain warmed up for improving overall memory, do the following brief awareness exercise.

→ EXERCISE **TEST YOUR MEMORY**

1 Get out your notebook and pen, and place them on the table. Then go into a different room (any room is fine).

2 Spend three to five minutes noticing everything you can about the room and your experience. Just let your eyes land on different areas of the room. Allow your mind to settle on any memories or feelings that come up.

3 Head back to your notebook and write down what sticks out the most to you. Was it items you saw in the room? Was it the lighting in the room? Was it scents or other sensations? Was it feelings or memories?

This exercise immerses you in the many layers of information that make up overall memories. You will also have practiced using awareness to notice and collect information—and focused awareness helps you retain information. As discussed at the beginning of this chapter, memories cannot be fully formed without adequate awareness or attention.

As important as attention and awareness are to creating memories, they are not the only factors that contribute to creating well-formed memories. Let's take a look at some additional factors that help make stronger, longer-lasting memories.

Evolution provided us with a valuable tool for making sure certain memories stick, and that tool is *emotion*. Emotionally charged events and information are some of the easiest to remember, and consequently the hardest to forget. Negative emotions tend to create the strongest memories. We all have examples of negative events that we wish we could forget—times when we were embarrassed, scared, or felt inadequate. As much as we would like to strike them from our mental record, it's just not going to happen. Those kinds of memories are extremely robust. Before the comfort of electricity, air conditioning, and grocery stores, it was critical to our survival to remember which plants would make us sick or the most likely place for a bear attack. Does this mean positive emotions won't make strong memories? No. However, you need to put in extra effort to boost your awareness of positive emotions in order to boost positive memories. If you only remember the times you messed up, then your self-image will start to be that of someone who only messes up. Make an extra effort to label positive experiences. Think of it as a highlighting marker for your life. Pat yourself on the back for being on time or getting things done early, for example, and reflect on why it went well.

Evolution also comes into play with writing and its role in consolidating memories. There's a reason why I've asked you to use a notebook for the exercises in this book, rather than a computer. We evolved with handwriting; therefore writing is the physical manifestation of learning. We will look at this again later in this chapter. For now, just note the fact that before written language, humans used pictographs to keep track of information and share knowledge. These are the drawings we see on cave walls and rock formations throughout the world, dating back over 10,000 years. Using writing implements to preserve memories is built into our evolutionary history. You, too, can use pictographs for improved memory. Simply making stick-figure drawings of events or information increases the likelihood that you will create strong memories, and you'll be able to use these drawings to help you remember later.

Another way to improve overall memory is to use metaphor. I remember the first evaluation I received as a college professor. I was commended for using a lot of analogy and metaphor in my lectures to illustrate the concepts I was teaching. It wasn't something I'd ever thought about before. It turned out that it's a great way to teach, because it helps students commit information to memory. That discovery piqued my interest enough to trace the origins of my own use of metaphor to aid memory. I found out from my mother that she always used metaphor to help me remember information in school. (Thanks, Mom!) But this trick isn't just for studying. You can use metaphor to improve your memory in day-to-day life. For example, maybe you have trouble remembering to write out the steps of a project before starting. You might want to use the metaphor of bread crumbs in the children's story of "Hansel and Gretel" to remind you. "I've got this huge project to do. I don't even know where to start. Oh, right, I need to lay bread crumbs to find my way." Or you could use the yellow brick road from *The Wizard of Oz*. "I don't even know how I'm going to get this done. Ahhh, yes, I need to follow the yellow brick road by writing out the steps in the project."

Let's look at some additional practical tips to help you improve your overall memory.

tip **Breathe when you forget.** If you have no memory of what you need to do or of an important piece of information, pause to take three slow breaths. It will reduce anxiety and improve your focus and ability to remember.

tip **Rehearse the information.** *Rehearsal* is a fancy term for repeating the information over and over in your mind. It helps commit the information to memory. For example, "Tell Suzie Dr. Brown wants to schedule for August 6. Schedule Dr. Brown for August 6. Dr. Brown August 6. Tell Suzie to schedule Dr. Brown for August 6." You probably already do this for things like phone numbers.

tip **Use mnemonics.** Mnemonics are patterns of letters that help with remembering words or concepts. For example, a way to remember the five Great Lakes is HOMES, for the lake names Huron, Ontario, Michigan, Erie, and Superior.

tip **Check your mind-set.** If you go into the process of trying to memorize information or trying to recall something, and already feel mentally beaten down, you will be in trouble. Instead, put your mental "game face" on: "All right, I've got this. I can memorize this," or "I can remember that. Give me a moment to use my awesome memory techniques."

TIE EMOTION AND METAPHOR TOGETHER

1 Reflect on your experience and think of a mistake you don't want to make but continue making anyway due to memory lapses. This could be something small, like leaving your shoes at the top of the stairs, or something big, like accidentally blowing off a boring meeting at work. Once you have something, write it down in your notebook.

2 Write down how you felt when the situation happened in the past. For example, "When I left my shoes at the top of the stairs, my spouse got very angry and told me I am putting the kids in danger of tripping and falling down the stairs. I felt like a bad parent, like I can't even do simple things. I felt sad and frustrated."

3 Create a metaphor for the repeated behavior. For example, "Skipping the boring meeting at work is getting me in trouble and might cost me my job and paycheck. It's like a kid refusing to eat three pieces of broccoli, causing her to lose her ice cream sundae. It's not worth it!"

MNEMONICS AND POWERFUL PICTOGRAPHS

1 Ask a friend or family member to tell you a story about a dream they have had recently or one they remember.

2 After they tell you the dream, either draw a simple line drawing (pictograph) or create a mnemonic of their dream in your notebook. Keep in mind that artistic ability is *not* important.

3 Two or three days later, use the pictograph or mnemonic to prompt your memory of the dream, and write down the contents of the dream. Read it or e-mail it to your friend and ask if it's accurate.

Remembering and Following Instructions

"Instructions" might as well be a four-letter word for people with ADHD—they typically really struggle with them. Instructions are forgotten, never heard, lost, followed out of order, and more. This leads to work and academic performance issues, as well as interpersonal conflict. I'm sure you have had many of those moments when you've sat down to do a project and realized you didn't know what to do and there was no one around to ask—or those moments when you worked incredibly hard on a project, only to find out you did it wrong. These situations chip away at your self-esteem and cause the people in your life to feel doubt and resentment toward you.

In my practice coaching people with ADHD, I write instructions down for the strategies we're covering, hand out printed instructions, or make sure clients write down my verbal instructions. The point is, without instructions to follow, the probability of success drops significantly. It's important that you learn methods to use whenever someone is giving you instructions or whenever you need to instruct yourself in carrying out a task. The idea of instructing yourself might sound a bit weird, but it's something we do all the time without even noticing it.

In this section, I will show you ways to capture instructions given to you, tips for following instructions, and how to create or reconstruct instructions if they have been lost or missed altogether.

So, here's the million-dollar question: What is the most important first step in capturing instructions being given to you? Any guesses? Come on, you've got this; there you go—it's *focus*! If there were such a thing as mental superglue, I would ask you to take the word *instructions* and the word *focus* and glue them together permanently. Whenever you hear someone say, "Okay, here's what I want you to do," "Please follow these steps," "In preparation for tomorrow's meeting . . . " or anything *at all* that signals instructions, directions, or requirements, I want you to think, "Time to focus!" Granted, focus has its own challenges, and we'll tackle that in the next sections of this chapter. For now, just remember to be on alert for any cue that you're about to receive instructions, and try to pay close attention to them.

Also, when you're about to get instructions and find yourself thinking, "Yeah, yeah, I've got it," or "I already know what to do," realize that you are likely creating a huge blind spot in your working memory. Never assume you know what the instructions will be, and don't overestimate your ability to retain even simple things. I'm sure you've been in a busy restaurant where the server didn't write down your order as you gave it. What tends to happen? Your order is often wrong, or the request made for extra sauce or no garlic didn't get followed. Don't fall into this trap in your work or home life. The "Yeah, I've got it" attitude can lead to serious mistakes and lots of wasted time.

Now that you're focused and ready to listen to my instructions, you can use the following tips to ensure success.

tip **Write down the instructions.** Seems like a no-brainer, but it's a corner people often cut. This is the rule of thumb for instructions and anything of importance: *If it's not written down, it doesn't exist.*

tip **Don't get lost in the details at first.** It would be wonderful if everyone gave an overview of instructions and then filled in the details, but that's not the norm. You will likely find instructions coming at you fast and with a ton of step-by-step detail. When the person giving instructions moves on to the next step in the instructions and you haven't written down all the nuts and bolts of the first step, just jump to the next step with them and start writing it down. You will be able to come back and fill in the missing information.

tip **Repeat and recap.** After the instructions have been given, ask the person to repeat them: "Okay, let me make sure I've got this. First I'm going to . . . Next I'm going to . . . " This is the time to fill in anything you missed. Sometimes you won't be able to write instructions down, which makes repeating and recapping critical.

tip **Give context and meaning to each aspect of the instructions.** People often know that a whole project or task is important but rarely give each step meaning and importance. Think back to when you were in high school math, and the teacher instructed you to show your work. If you were like me, you probably thought this was ridiculous and didn't bother. In fact, it turns out to be an important part of the process because it's how the teacher can tell if you have a full understanding of the concept.

tip **Instruct yourself.** It doesn't really matter whether you weren't given instructions, lost them, or didn't write them down. You still need to do the project. A helpful way to come up with instructions for yourself is to first outline the steps as best you can and then fill in the instructions. A good way to fill in instructions is to think of previous tasks you've done that are similar and draw on them for information. Another way to fill in the blanks is to ask a friend or colleague. If no one is available, you might find the information on the Internet. Careful though: The web is a black hole of distractions.

tip **Instruct someone else.** If you are without instructions and feeling anxious, it can help to make it about someone else. Pretend someone is sitting next to you and they need to do the same project. Try giving this fictitious person instructions to follow. You just might have more knowledge than you realize.

EXERCISE FINDING FOCUS AND RETAINING INSTRUCTIONS

By doing this exercise, you will be pushing your ability to focus to the limit. You'll need to use one or more of the tips in this section to complete it successfully. You may find you are not able to complete it, but that's okay. The goal of this exercise is to practice writing down instructions in a highly distracting environment.

1 Find an instructional cooking video online that is between 5 and 15 minutes long.

2 Get out your notebook and pen to write down the instructions given in the video.

3 Plug a pair of earbuds or headphones into a separate device (e.g., smartphone). Place one earbud in one ear, or adjust the headphones so only one ear is covered. Play some sort of distracting music that you don't like in that ear.

4 Play the cooking video on a separate device (e.g., laptop), with the volume on so your other ear can hear it.

5 Without pausing the video at any point, write down the instructions. It will be hard, but it's supposed to be.

EXERCISE CREATING INSTRUCTIONS FROM SCRATCH

1 Ask a friend or family member to assign you a complex task. You are not actually going to do it, so the specific task isn't important. They might direct you to chop firewood, bake a cake, or create a spreadsheet.

2 Check your anxiety level, and take three slow breaths if you need to. It will help with focus and clarity of thought.

3 Break the task down into steps, essentially creating an outline for the instructions. You may need to remember similar tasks you have done previously in order to create the outline. Really try to stretch yourself before going online to find instructions.

4 Fill in each section of the outline with more detailed instructions. Don't be afraid to trust your intuition.

5 Show your instructions to the person and ask them if they are correct, based on the task they assigned to you. Were your instructions accurate? Would they work if actually implemented?

Managing Common Distractions

The most common symptom for anyone with ADHD is difficulty with regulating attention. Interestingly, the name Attention Deficit Hyperactivity Disorder is fairly misleading, especially for adults. People with ADHD don't really have a *deficit* in attention; in a way, they have *too much* attention. The struggle lies in their ability to regulate *where* their attention is focused and for how long. Most adults with ADHD are very familiar with feeling either totally scattered or locked in deep focus on a single task. Unfortunately, that deep hyperfocus is not very predictable and is not always directed at the right task. Also, most adults with ADHD don't experience hyperactivity. Hyperactivity tends to fade away in adulthood.

The way in which ADHD affects directed attention can actually be an asset in many circumstances. People with ADHD can often come up with many novel ideas, for example. As someone who has spent his whole career in Silicon Valley, I can tell you with certainty that the ability to come up with ideas has made many adults with ADHD very wealthy—so there's an upside to the condition. The problems people encounter are often centered around initiating and sustaining focus over the long haul to see their ideas manifest. I really like adult-ADHD specialist and author Dr. Dale Archer's tagline, "What you thought was a diagnosis may be your greatest strength." For successful people like the founder of Virgin Records and Virgin Airlines, Richard Branson, it's true. However, most people find their ADHD to be part of a daily battle. At the forefront of that battle are distractions.

Distractions are absolutely everywhere, but they don't always affect us the same way. What may be a big distraction one day is not on another day, and vice versa. Various factors play into how distractible we are at any given time, ranging from our stress level to the type of activity requiring attention. One class of distractions that doesn't get mentioned enough is *internal* distractions. These are thoughts and feelings that originate inside a person. Remember, from an evolutionary standpoint, negative thoughts and emotions are supposed to capture attention and be hard to block out. Thoughts about other tasks that need to be done, previous bad experiences, daydreams, ideas, and so on, are all self-created internal distractions that can get in the way.

Fortunately, there are tried-and-true methods for managing all types of distractions. Here are some of my top tips for managing distractions.

tip **Keep your digital devices in check.** The most common sources of distraction today are smartphones, tablets, and computers. When you sit down to focus on a task, it's imperative that you turn off all notifications, turn off chat programs, close your e-mail, and close extra browser tabs. If you struggle to keep certain websites or apps under control when you need to focus, you can download one of the many "blocking" apps, such as Self-Control for Mac OS, StayFocusd extension for Chrome, or Blacklist for smartphones.

tip **Use a distraction log.** I find this simple tool to be invaluable. I even used it while writing this book. The distraction log is a dedicated blank piece of paper or notebook that you keep next to you when working. Whenever an idea, a persistent thought, or something important to do or remember pops into your mind, write it in the distraction log and move on. It functions like a journal in releasing the thought from your mind and like a safety net in catching important thoughts and ideas you'll want to return to later.

tip **Stay clear on the task at hand.** Before you get a task under-
way, make sure you are operating with what I call "mindful
intention." This means you have spent time mindfully reflecting on
what task needs to get done, and you are now intentionally acting.
If you often follow distractions and struggle to recall what task you
were working on, you can write the name of the task on a sticky note
and place it on your computer or in your work area.

tip **Blow away distractions, literally.** When you are in a focused
state, you have a very rhythmic and consistent breathing
pattern, inhaling and exhaling with plenty of air. When you are
anxious, tense, or distracted, your breathing becomes shallow and
erratic. When you feel distraction creeping in, especially thought-
based distractions, that's your cue to start taking slow, full breaths
in and out. Within moments, your ability to focus will improve.

tip **Noise-canceling headphones.** There's not much to explain here.
If your environment permits it, you can use noise-canceling
headphones, with or without music.

tip **Block distraction with another distraction.** This is not a riddle
or trick. Using music to block out external noise can have the
extra bonus of putting a pep in your step while working. Most people
find music with a consistent beat and few to no lyrics the best for
focus. Probably one of the best sources for this type of music is Alex
Cruz, a popular DJ who produces music with very consistent beat
patterns that seem to fall in many people's sweet spot. It's also a nice
bonus that his music is available online for free.

PRACTICE MAKES PERFECT

The goal of this exercise is to practice using the tips above during a task that's already easy for you to focus on. An example for me is editing and adjusting photographs. I am an avid photographer, and being in the digital age, I edit my photos on a computer and don't struggle to focus on it at all. What's something you can work on that's easy for you to focus on?

1 Choose a task you already find easy to focus on.

2 Find a location that's fairly distracting. This may be a coffee shop, your office, or even your home with kids or roommates present.

3 Locate a dedicated distraction log (see tip #2) and place it at your workstation.

4 Start working on your chosen task. After about 10 minutes of work, move on to step 5.

5 Intentionally allow a couple of distracting thoughts to come up. There are two ways to do this. You can simply let yourself become aware of the noise around you and think something like, "Ugh, this is a distracting place. I'll never get anything done." Or you may think about a project at work or home that you need to do. Make an extra effort to think about some of the outstanding tasks for the project. I recommend noticing the distractions around you *and* triggering thoughts about a project to get the most practice from this exercise.

6 Use rhythmic breathing (see tip #4) to calm your mind and help put you in a more focused state.

7 Write down in the distraction log the name of the project and the tasks you thought of.

8 Get back to work on the original (easy to focus on) task.

9 In your notebook, write a brief reflection on your experience. Were you able to use the breathing and distraction log techniques? Did the techniques help you get back to work?

After completing this exercise, you may choose to do it again for practice, or you may just start using the techniques in your daily life. Whatever is most comfortable for you is best. I want you to begin trusting your intuition and allowing your confidence to build.

How to Sustain Attention

To sustain your attention, it can be very helpful to *use* the traits and behavioral patterns that come with ADHD rather than fight against them. One trait that's common to nearly all people with ADHD is the desire to seek novelty. One way to create novelty in your work is to mix things up by not working on the same project all day long. Granted, there are times when you must grind away on the same project all day, but hopefully, it's not the norm. Lack of novelty often leads to boredom, and boredom leads to distraction—so it helps to mix things up.

EXERCISE BREAK UP TASKS

My wife is an Olympic-trained soccer player and an incredibly driven person. After our first child was born, she decided to run her first marathon. I remember waiting at the finish line for her. I'd seen people come across the finish line who were in terrible shape: crying, shaking, vomiting—it was crazy! Then here comes my wife, smiling, barely even breaking a sweat. I asked her how she finished so fast and with such a positive mood. After all, running 26.2 miles in warm weather in under a few hours is no small feat. She told me she just focused on one mile at a time; she treated each mile as its own little race. I still think that's genius.

For this exercise, I want you to practice breaking up a couple of large tasks into smaller pieces. This will let you mix up your tasks on any given day. Intentionally task switching in order to foster novelty can be hard if it's not clear to you when to pause one task and switch to another, so practicing this exercise will help.

1 Decide on two tasks or projects that will each take many hours to complete.

2 Look at each task and identify where you can place breaks that will allow you to stop and switch to the other task. For example, I usually read a couple of nonfiction books at any given time. I like to switch back and forth between them to keep from getting bored. It works well, because books have chapters that create natural places to stop. Can you break up your project like a chapter in a book? You want to break it up in a way that makes it easy to return to at another time.

3 Write down these "chapters" or breaks for each project in your notebook or in a document on your computer for use when you sit down to work for an extended period of time.

> **tip** **Chunking time, taking breaks.** Contrary to what many college students seem to believe, it's not "normal" or effective to work for many hours on a task without a break. When people don't take breaks, it leads to mental fatigue. Mental fatigue hurts performance in all people and leads to increased distractibility for adults with ADHD. According to my friend Steven Kotler, an elite performance expert and director of research at the Flow Genome Project, all people need to take a break at about 90 minutes. Kotler says this break allows the brain to replenish the very important neurotransmitters needed for focus and productivity. The break needs to be an actual break. Simply stopping working on your taxes to surf social media and e-mail doesn't count. During the break, you should get up, walk, stretch, meditate briefly, hydrate, or do something else different from what you were doing.

CREATE A DAILY SCHEDULE

1 Think about how you can structure your daily routine to use both breaking up tasks and chunking time or taking breaks.

2 In your notebook, write down a schedule for tomorrow that you can follow. Make sure to include the blocks of time for work and the breaks for rest and rebuilding.

3 Follow your plan tomorrow. At the end of the day, reflect on the experience and identify any changes or adjustments you want to make for the next day.

4 Repeat steps 2 and 3 for the following day.

The Long Haul

Achieving focus for minutes or hours is one thing, but maintaining a broader focus over days or weeks is another. I'm not talking about literally staying focused in one sitting for days or weeks. I'm talking about staying engaged and progressing on projects and tasks that take days, weeks, or even months to complete.

In order to become consistently able to focus on and complete big projects, you must become skilled at project planning and use the skills you learned in the preceding sections in the moment to boost your focus. Skills such as minimizing distractions from digital devices, conscious breathing, keeping an eye on negative self-talk, using a distraction log, and operating with mindful intention should be in your toolbox all the time. As we've just seen, breaking up longer projects into smaller chunks boosts focus as well. However, in order to bring long projects to completion, you'll need to take the skill of breaking up your projects one step further.

Here's my favorite technique for managing projects over time. Say you need to paint your whole home. It's easy to procrastinate when faced with this type of large project, and it's easy to lose motivation. If you think about the project as one large task, "paint my whole home," it's overwhelming. The trick is to break it into smaller subtasks, and when I say smaller, I mean *really small*. Start by breaking the task down into three tiers.

- Tier 1 is the complete project, reflected in a target completion date.
- Tier 2 is the large chunks and their target completion dates.
- Tier 3 is the smaller subtasks that, together, make up the large chunks.

Let's stick with the painting example. Say you have four rooms to paint in four weeks, and your target completion date is June 30.

Tier 1: Paint all four rooms by June 30.

Tier 2:
- Chunk 1: Purchase paint and supplies by June 7.
- Chunk 2: Prep rooms for painting by June 14.
- Chunk 3: Paint rooms by June 30.

Tier 3:
- Chunk 1: (Purchase paint and supplies by June 7)
  - Review paint color options on June 1.
  - Measure square footage of rooms on June 3.
  - Create list of all supplies needed on June 5.
  - Purchase all paint and supplies at hardware store on June 7.

- Chunk 2: (Prep rooms for painting by June 14)
  - Remove or cover all furniture and paintings by June 10.
  - And continue in this way, adding all steps to prep the rooms by June 14.

By now, you should see that the project is much more manageable. The subtasks are also much easier to keep track of. In the example, you would create subtasks for the other two chunks of the project. Finally, it's very helpful to input all three tiers into your calendar and set reminders for the associated tasks. With smartphones and tablets, it's pretty easy to set reminders, for as far into the future as necessary. But don't overdo it with reminders, as they can lose their effectiveness if you have too many. No one likes bells and whistles coming from their devices all day long.

EXERCISE TRACK YOUR PROGRESS

After using the skill just covered to break down one of your projects or tasks into manageable pieces with target dates for each chunk, you will want to track your progress.

1 In your notebook, create a list of the tiers and chunks of the project. Try to write each on just one line.

2 For this step, you can choose one of two methods. You can create a small box to the left of each tier and chunk of the project, and use this box to check off each completed task. The other option is often the most popular and satisfying. Instead of using a check box, use your pen to draw a single line through each task. Most of my clients find it more satisfying to cross it out. However, don't scribble or make a mess, as you might want to be able to read it later if a double check is needed.

3 On a separate page in your notebook, write down all the positive thoughts, feelings, and rewards that came from completing sections of the project. I recommend doing it as you go, in a list. How it looks isn't important; it's just important to capture the thoughts, feelings, or rewards in the moment.

tip **Always write things down!** By following the rule of thumb that nothing exists unless you write it down, you will save valuable mental resources by not having to decide *what* to write down. This is not just for tasks. Any ideas that come to you, information to remember, and so on should get written down in your notebook. Use the notebook as a safety net to catch everything.

tip **Set up a reward system.** Decide on a reward that motivates you. It might be something you have wanted to do or buy. Whatever it is should be reasonable in value in relation to the task. If you complete the task by the decided date, give yourself your chosen reward. You can add another layer to this by having a "bonus prize" or a "runner up" prize (which should be something much smaller) that you give yourself if you complete more than half of the task by the deadline.

In the next chapter, you'll learn how to tackle and complete tasks by improving your organizational, planning, and time management skills.

Takeaways

- Exercise helps keep your brain fit and your memory sharp.
- Sleep is vitally important.
- Take three deep breaths when you have forgotten something to reduce anxiety, boost focus, and improve your ability to remember.
- If it's not written down, it doesn't exist. This is especially true for instructions.
- Instructions don't have to be perfectly written down.
- Recapping instructions helps them stick in your working memory.
- You can re-create lost instructions by pretending you are instructing someone else.
- To focus, shut off all digital distractions.
- Using a distraction log to capture ideas and information that pop into your mind helps you maintain focus on a task.
- Breaking up tasks into manageable chunks lessens overwhelm and procrastination.
- A daily schedule helps keep you on track.

3 Learn to Organize and Plan

Overview

ADHD symptoms have a way of turning into vicious cycles that keep the symptoms going, wreaking havoc on your quality of life. This is especially true of symptoms related to organizing, planning, managing your time, and completing tasks.

As we saw in chapter 2, projects that are not organized in clear steps can feel overwhelming, which can lead you to avoid them. The same is true of planning—when a task isn't adequately planned, it can feel impossible to get started. These are common symptoms that can lead to dramatic increases in procrastination.

I'm sure that at some point in your life, you have procrastinated on a task due to poor planning. The next thing you know, e-mails and calls start coming in, asking you for an update. This kicks off negative emotions like fear, anxiety, and shame. Rather than attend to the requests, you avoid them, which leaves you feeling more fear, anxiety, and shame. The further past the deadline you go, the worse things get. Now you are at your desk, gripped with negative emotions and unable to focus on any of your work. Before you realize it, you've wasted even more time avoiding the task. Finally, your boss gives you an ultimatum to get the task done ASAP or face the consequences. So, rather than planning mindfully and acting intentionally, you blow everything else off and dive deep into the task. By the time you finish, countless other tasks have backed up, and the cycle repeats. This time, it's much worse. You are more anxious, you are getting down on yourself, and your performance plummets along with your self-esteem. Such a nightmare—and it all could have been avoided.

In this chapter, you will learn strategies to improve the way you organize projects, plan tasks, manage your time, and keep track of it all. Once these systems are in place, you will be more productive and less stressed, and you will feel better about yourself. That's how you create a *virtuous* cycle.

How Organized Are You?

This is not a rhetorical or trick question. Even the most disorganized people have some level of organization. Like most things in life, organization is a continuum. Someone might say they don't get any exercise, because they don't intentionally work out or set aside time for fitness. But when you take a closer look, it becomes clear that they painted the garage, mowed the lawn, or chased a toddler around the house. Those types of tasks require physical activity that can be considered exercise. Organization is no different.

In my office, I treat many couples. Most of the time, only one person in the couple has ADHD, so I help them bridge the gap between their different approaches. One issue that comes up over and over is piles: piles of papers, piles of projects, piles of folded laundry—you name it. The interesting thing is that the person with ADHD, who creates the piles, often knows what's in each pile and can actually find things. But the piles wreak havoc on the general organization and cleanliness of the home. The piles are a version of organization, just not a very good one.

Everyone needs an organized and orderly environment. Even if you feel that your cluttered desk is not a problem, it is. Our minds tend to work overtime in cluttered environments in order to stay focused. Clutter and mess also tend to increase our anxiety. According to research conducted at UCLA, living in cluttered environments increases the release of the stress hormone cortisol. Clutter, piles, disorganization, and other forms of chaos create stimuli that the brain must contend with.

Before starting to write this, I removed all clutter and unneeded items from my desk. I wanted to focus on my computer and my notes—that's it. I even decided to run a little experiment in preparation for this chapter. On two occasions this week, I intentionally left cluttered papers, extra books, and other unneeded items on the desk. It was eye-opening! I was not able to work as efficiently. I kept experiencing writer's block while my mind worked overtime to block out the mess. When I removed the clutter, *boom!* Just like that, I was back in business, ready to write.

So now that I have your attention, how organized are you?

EXERCISE WHERE'S YOUR STUFF?

This exercise will help you be more aware of your level of organization at work or home.

1 Choose two separate areas that you use for work or for completing tasks. Examples are your desk (at work or home), your kitchen counter, tables, and so on. Once you have identified them, write the two areas down in your notebook, leaving a few lines of space below each one.

2 Go to one of the areas you selected in step 1. Stand or sit at the location and simply look at all the items present. This is fairly clear if you are at your desk but might not be as clear if you work at home at a table or kitchen counter. The key is to observe everything on the desk, counter, table, and so on.

3 In your notebook, under the name of the area, write down all the items that don't belong there or are not necessary for the tasks you tend to do there. If you start wanting to rationalize or make excuses for why certain things are there, it's a pretty good indicator that it

does not belong there. This is a bit like drinking alcohol. If your doctor asks you how much you drink and one of your immediate reactions is to explain why you have five drinks a night, then you probably shouldn't be having five drinks a night. If you need to explain to yourself why your son's broken toy has been on your kitchen counter for three years waiting to be glued, it does not belong there.

4 Repeat steps 2 and 3 for the second area you chose.

5 Turn to a fresh page in your notebook and write down your reflections on the experience. Were there many things that didn't belong? Did you feel embarrassed by some of the items because of how out of place they were? Did you feel good about removing them? What have you learned about your space that you want to remember?

EXERCISE WHAT'S YOUR PLAN?

The goal of this exercise is to help you gauge your ability to organize a project or task. During many of these exercises, I have given you instructions like, "Get out your notebook and open it to a fresh page." When I give you instructions like that, I am organizing your plan for you. Adults with ADHD often find themselves repeatedly distracted due to lack of planning. They get fired up when they start a project, only to realize they need to go look for information or supplies. It's hard to reengage in the project and find focus after the interruptions. Every time you step away or shift focus off the project, you increase the risk of getting pulled into a rabbit hole of distractions. Rabbit holes are a hassle. Before you know it, your afternoon has been spent organizing photos in the garage when you needed to be doing your taxes.

Let's get started.

1 Find a place at home or work with very few distractions. You are going to be thinking fast and will need to pay good attention.

2 Decide on three projects or tasks you want to do, and write them down at the top of a blank page. They can be work related, such as producing a revenue report or building a cabinet, or they can be home related, such as cooking spaghetti or helping your child with a school project.

3 Turn to a fresh page in your notebook.

4 For the first project or task, write down the steps you must take before getting started. This might include supplies you need, an environment that needs to be prepared, instructions that need to be found, and so on. Do your best to write them down as fast as you can.

5 Repeat steps 3 and 4 for the next project or task until you have done this for all three projects.

6 Evaluate your work and write down a reflection in your notebook. Were you easily able to identify a preparation plan? Is anything missing? Did you have any insights or "aha" moments?

tip **The joys of weeding!** When you complete a task or project, make sure to throw or put away any materials, notes, supplies, alerts, and so on that were associated with it. This will help you reduce clutter and be less distracted when you start another task.

Get Going: Task Initiation

One of the most common things I hear from new clients or participants at my workshops is that they have trouble starting tasks. You may have become a pro at planning your projects, but you still struggle to actually get started. There are so many consequences to putting off tasks or getting distracted, ranging from poor performance at work to missed opportunities to increased stress to lack of self-confidence.

I have good news. Since most of the barriers that prevent you from getting started are psychological or emotional in nature, they can be managed. Once you identify that a particular struggle is based in your own thoughts or emotions, you can use proven methods to take the stress out of starting tasks and give you the power to initiate on demand.

CONFRONTING PROCRASTINATION

Procrastination—putting off a task until a later time—is typically an act of avoidance. You might avoid doing something because it's boring, you're afraid of failing, you're a perfectionist, or you're feeling overwhelmed. Unfortunately, avoidance breeds more avoidance. The further away from the task you get, the harder it is to get started. It's a nasty cycle that can drive your stress levels through the roof.

EXERCISE WHAT ARE YOU AVOIDING?

This brief assessment will give you an idea of what type of procrastinator you are.

1 Draw a line down the middle of a blank page in your notebook so you have two columns.

2 In the left column, create a list of 5 to 10 projects and tasks you are currently procrastinating about or have procrastinated about in the last few months.

3 In the right column, write down the main reason you avoided or are avoiding that task.

EXAMPLE

PROJECT/TASK	REASON FOR PROCRASTINATION
Do my taxes	It's boring
Mow the lawn	I hate the mess
Call Uncle Tim	He is a snore and repeats himself
Buy a suit	Can't find the time
Get bids from contractor	I'm afraid they will rip me off
Find a therapist	I don't even know where to start

4 Review the two columns. Are there reasons for your avoidance that are listed several times? Are there types of tasks that you tend to avoid?

From this, you can get a pretty quick idea of what type of procrastinator you are. Are you mainly a perfectionist? Do you primarily get overwhelmed? Are you chiefly anxious or fearful? Do you mainly fall victim to self-doubt?

Once you know the type of procrastinator you are, you can be more aware of your avoidance and be ready to change course.

tip **Use a timer.** Instead of struggling against time, get time on your side. Focus on working for 20 minutes. Simply set a kitchen timer, a small digital timer, or a timer app on your computer or phone for 20 minutes. During that time, work on the project or task at hand. When the timer goes off, take a five-minute break to go to the restroom, take a short walk, or something similar. *Do not start surfing the web or go on social media.* At the end of five minutes, set the timer for 20 more minutes and get back to work. If you don't feel like continuing, that's okay. After all, 20 minutes of focused work is better than no work at all.

Get Your Priorities Straight

As important as prioritization is, it remains one of the most elusive skills for adults with ADHD. There are many reasons for this, but the biggest offenders are typically a lack of prioritization techniques and very little awareness of priorities in general. As you will see in the next section, adults with ADHD tend to work on whatever is presented to them at the time.

Take a moment to think about your daily experience. How often do you decide what your top priority is? How often do you decide ahead of time what you are going to work on? Do you have a framework for understanding what should be a priority? If you are like most adults with ADHD, you probably find yourself in "firefighter mode" a lot. When you are constantly behind and putting out fires, it can seem impossible to prioritize. You likely work on whatever task comes your way then and there. But the task that is catching your attention is not necessarily the right one to work on now.

In the next section, we will address pesky tasks and people who seem to gobble up all your time. For now, I'm going to arm you with a few simple methods for prioritizing your tasks.

LEARN TO TRIAGE

Mention *triage* in a room full of doctors and you will immediately get everyone's attention, and for good reason. The term is used when there are multiple patients needing care and decisions need to be made about who needs treatment urgently. Triage is used in emergency rooms and war-zone hospitals where there are multiple emergencies unfolding at once. Sound familiar? I bet it does. ADHD has a way of creating a need to triage the multiple outstanding projects and their associated crises.

Becoming good at prioritizing based on urgency is an important skill for everyone with ADHD. This can be particularly challenging due to the unpredictable nature of attention that comes with ADHD. Some days, everything can seem like an emergency. In fact, the sense that everything is an emergency is so common that it can become your default state, even when there isn't an emergency.

You will have the greatest success if you decide which tasks are the most urgent *before* you find yourself in a crisis. After all, trying to decide what is urgent while reading a barrage of e-mails and fielding calls in the morning is very hard. The best way is to decide each afternoon or evening which task for the next day is the most urgent. If you end up with two equally urgent tasks, you should do your least favorite one first. If you get it out of the way first, you will feel relieved, and the sense of accomplishment will give you momentum for the next task.

SET YOUR GOALS

Luckily, you don't need to put out a fire every day. But each day has tasks that need to get done, whether you are at work or at home. In order to get everything done, it's important to set goals on a daily basis. You might have goals that carry over from the day before, and that's okay.

When deciding on your daily goals, it's helpful to put them into three categories: "must do," "should do," and "would be nice to do." Once you fill the three categories with goals, you can prioritize them within each category. (After doing this, you may find that there are several fires to put out and you need to triage [see page 53].)

tip **Assign priority levels to your goals.** Tasks that belong in the "must do" category are those that are time sensitive or those where someone else is counting on you and will be upset if you don't deliver. Here are some examples:

- Turning in your taxes on time
- Delivering a report that your boss needs for an afternoon meeting
- Picking up a prescription for a loved one

Tasks that belong in the "should do" category are those that will become time sensitive in the near future or those that are valuable to you because they will help advance your career, relationship, or agenda. Here are some examples:

- Preparing documents for your accountant
- Making calls to prospective customers
- Scheduling a doctor's appointment

Tasks that belong in the "would be nice to do" category are those that are not urgent. Maybe they are connected to a leisure activity or are not related to anything in the "must do" or "should do" categories. Here are some examples:

- Organizing your work space
- Setting up a networking lunch for the near future
- Finding a hotel for your upcoming vacation

EXERCISE HELP A FRIEND PRIORITIZE

It's often easier to help someone else, because you don't have the same level of investment or emotional connection to their situation.

1 Ask a friend or family member if you can practice some new prioritization techniques with them.

2 Have them tell you or e-mail you a list of 10 to 15 tasks they need to accomplish. This should be a mix of tasks from all areas in their life (work, personal, family, and so on).

3 Once you have the list, ask them questions about each task to determine which category it should go in. Ask them about due dates and timelines, who is counting on them, and other factors, such as hours of operation or time zones, that may affect the outcomes.

4 Place each of their tasks into the three categories ("must do," "should do," and "would be nice to do"). Then ask them for feedback about how you prioritized the tasks. If they agree with how you did it, ask them why they agree. If they don't agree with how you did it, ask them why they disagree. Doing this will allow you to uncover considerations you missed and reinforce what you did right.

Time Management

Whether your ADHD symptoms cause you to be late, lose track of time, misjudge how long things take, or struggle to fit everything into your day, it all has to do with your core mental skills. Remember that all those skills—like planning, paying attention, scheduling, managing emotions, setting goals, and organizing—live in the part of your brain most affected by ADHD. You likely experience moments when the clock ticks by in slow motion, and other times when it shoots by like a rocket. Difficulty with time management can lead to some of the biggest frustrations for you and those close to you.

STEALING BACK YOUR TIME

It's easy to beat yourself up for all these time management issues; and you are free to keep doing that, but it will only make things worse. How can you focus on doing things differently when you are busy beating yourself up? Also, it's just not your fault. Digital devices like smartphones and tablets eat up your time. Activities like consuming media and shopping suck up your time. Work hungrily gobbles up your time. Before you know it, you are out of time, haven't completed a single thing, and are stressed to the max.

In order to address the issue of time management, I have broken it into four parts:

- Awareness of time
- Digital devices/media consumption
- Tasks at work or home
- People

As you have seen in earlier chapters, awareness is the first step toward making change. I find that most people with ADHD struggle with the concept of time—that is, they struggle with projecting how long it takes to finish a task or get somewhere. Before everyone had a cell phone in their pocket, it was normal to wear a watch. Now, most people check their phones to tell the time. There are two big issues with this: One, the phone is a shiny box of distractions. You may use it to check the time and end up spending an hour texting or answering e-mails. The second issue is your awareness of time. Digital clocks (just digits) don't allow for the spatial awareness of time that analog (dials and hands) clocks have. To be fair, I didn't come up with this idea. When we were kids, my dad always made sure we had an analog watch, because he wanted us to learn about time awareness. (Thanks, Dad!) When you wear an analog watch, you can look at it not only to see the exact time but also to start developing visual awareness of time. You begin to see an hour in parts, like pieces of a pie. This is where "half past the hour" and "it's about a quarter to two" come from.

Digital devices are a double-edged sword for people with ADHD. Smartphones can be very helpful for setting reminders or having your calendar in your pocket at all times. However, everything that makes everyone you know get hooked on their digital devices also affects you, but at a much stronger level. Whenever you pull your phone out to check an e-mail, read a text, look at social media, or play a game, you release a hit of the reward chemical dopamine in your brain. Dopamine not only gives you the sense of reward, but also allows you to decide what task to do, where to focus, and what goals to work toward. Additionally, dopamine is one of the main driving forces behind all addictions, and adults with ADHD tend to have an increased risk of addiction. So when the lack of impulse control and reduced ability to focus are combined with the increased risk of addiction due to a lack of dopamine, people with ADHD can more easily end up with an addiction to digital devices.

Digital devices also decrease your ability to focus for extended periods of time. It's very rare for anyone to use their smartphone to do one sustained task. You probably know exactly what I mean. In a five-minute period, you might check your text messages and e-mail, check social media, look at your calendar, scan some photos, watch the first minute of a funny video, and ultimately forget why you got the phone out in the first place. This pattern gets reinforced by doing it over and over, which makes it harder for you to direct your attention when you need to. Doing this in the morning has the compounded effect of putting your mind in a distracted state first thing, and it will plague you all day.

It's very important to have all your tasks written down in a list. Most people hate lists at first, but I will show you a way to make lists your friend. You can also exercise awareness by pausing during a task to ask yourself if you are doing what you are supposed to be doing, or if what you are doing is getting you closer to your goal.

Finally, people can eat up your time. The most common reason is because you let them! I find that most people with ADHD tend to say yes to requests too often. Maybe self-doubt leads you to anxiously say, "Yes, I can do it." Or the task someone is asking you to do is more enticing than what you are currently doing. Either way, you end up taking on too much and ultimately letting people down by not completing anything.

Another way people eat up your time is through interruptions. People who don't have ADHD are better at switching between tasks or stopping what they are doing to answer a question. But people with ADHD need consistent focus with few interruptions. It's important to start practicing saying no. You can do this by evaluating your ability to take on projects and by keeping track of what you're working on if you get interrupted.

A helpful way to address the "saying yes" problem is to use the acronym PET: pause, evaluate, trust. When someone asks you to do something, first *pause*. This can simply be putting your hand on your chin and looking away in thought or saying, "Hmm, let me think for a moment." During that pause, *evaluate* your current workload to decide if you can actually fit it in. People would rather have you say, "I'm sorry, but I just can't take that on right now," than say yes and not deliver. Finally, you need to *trust* yourself. If you have paused and evaluated adequately, there's no need for self-doubt. Trust yourself. It feels good. The more you are able to take on things you can really accomplish, the more you will get done, and the more confident you and others will become in your abilities.

EXERCISE MANAGE MEDIA AND DEVICES

The best way to manage your time around smartphones, tablets, and so on is to improve your self-control.

By doing this exercise, you will develop a better awareness of two things: You will have a sense of how much self-control you have around your phone, and you will become aware of the thoughts and feelings it provokes. In the future, when you are focusing on a task, having dinner with a friend, or just wanting a break from media, notice these thoughts and feelings and recognize them as your mind playing tricks on you. Let them pass. For example, if you think, "I'm feeling anxious," "I'm feeling like I'm missing out," or "I want to check my phone really badly!" just say to yourself, "Those are just silly thoughts and feelings. I'm okay. I'll just keep focusing on what I'm doing." The more you do this, the easier it will get.

1 Make yourself uncomfortable.

2 Take your phone or tablet out. Send a text to a bunch of friends, coworkers, or family members asking them a simple question. The question is not important; just ask something that people are likely to respond to fairly quickly.

3 Turn the ringer and notification volume on your phone all the way up. Then set it facedown in front of you.

4 Begin working on a task you find boring.

5 When the phone buzzes, beeps, or rings, *do not pick it up*. Leave it facedown for as long as you can.

6 Write down how long you were able to hold out before picking it up. Also write down any thoughts or feelings that came up.

tip **The Cannibal Task.** The Cannibal Task is one that gradually eats up big chunks of your time—time that really belongs to other tasks—over a period of days or weeks. This most often happens with tasks that don't have clear parameters. Don't allow vague tasks or tasks without hard deadlines to drag out endlessly and eat you alive. If you are given a task that doesn't have clear steps, break it down yourself (see page 37). If you are given a task that doesn't have a clear deadline, create a deadline. More time does not equal better work. Break it down, set deadlines, and get it done.

Your Daily To-Dos

If you have a history of losing your to-do lists or you feel like a failure for not completing everything on your list, you might have negative associations with lists. I find that many adults with ADHD often feel as if their list were a teacher, parent, or coach hovering over them and triggering shame. But you can change that association and learn to excel with the help of a basic system.

The list is actually your friend. High achievers in all areas of life use lists. Keeping track of tasks and determining their priority is essential to getting things done and reaching goals. Mental skills are important for all people, not just those with ADHD. I've spent time looking into the habits of highly successful people, and they have one thing in common: Daily lists are one of their most important tools.

WHY MAKE A DAILY LIST?

Remember: *If it's not written down, it doesn't exist.* By treating *every* task as something to be written down, you won't waste precious mental resources trying to decide whether or not to write it down. From picking up milk on your way home to turning in your expense reports, it all goes on the list. *If it's not written down, it doesn't exist.*

Along with helping you complete your tasks, be more productive, and reach your goals, lists act as a safety net and an extension of your awareness. If everything goes on the list, tasks won't get dropped, like how a safety net catches trapeze artists if they fall. Checking your list daily brings tasks into your awareness, greatly increasing the likelihood they will get done.

In order to make lists effective and less scary, I recommend following a few principles:

- Use a notebook like the one you are using for the exercises in this book. I find that a notebook about the size of a passport is best.

- Keep your list tidy. A cluttered mess is visually overwhelming and hard to use. Write each item on one or two lines and then skip a line before writing the next task. Leaving a blank line makes things easier to see and allows room for adding information if you need to.

- Give yourself the satisfaction of crossing out completed tasks. A single line through a completed task tends to trigger a sense of reward. Don't scribble it out—that's messy, and you may need to go back later to see if you completed a task.

- Keep adding to your list by putting new tasks at the end of it. If someone asks you for something, write it down at the end of the list. If you remember that you need to schedule a doctor's appointment, write it down.

- Rewrite your list and prioritize it daily (see page 54). By taking just a few minutes a day to carry over tasks from the day before in order of priority, you will be a step ahead of many people. Just as we saw earlier in the chapter, deciding the one or two "must do" tasks for each day will help you stay on top of things and meet your deadlines. Rewriting the list daily also helps bring the tasks into your awareness.

- Watch out for negative self-talk. If you look at the list and beat yourself up for not having finished everything or for having too many tasks, you will start to avoid the list. You don't need to complete everything on the list every day. You just need to complete the one or two "must do" tasks. Be kind to yourself.

TALKING WITH COWORKERS ABOUT ADHD

Not all work environments are created equal. It is true that ADHD typically falls into a class of conditions that have certain legal protections in the workplace (check the laws where you live). Unfortunately, bringing up your ADHD with some coworkers and bosses is more of a headache than it's worth. For example, in a casual conversation, you tell your boss that you have ADHD, and then every time you are late due to traffic or your project is erased due to a computer crash, it might be blamed on your ADHD rather than the actual cause. Most coworkers and bosses don't have a clear understanding of ADHD. It's not necessarily their fault—most doctors who are not specialists don't have a clear understanding of it either. You need to decide whether mentioning it in the workplace is right for you.

If you decide to discuss it at work, it's often best to have a direct conversation based on facts. You might want to discuss it if you have come up with a creative way of managing it and want to explain your technique. Maybe you decide to talk about ADHD because you need an accommodation such as noise-canceling headphones or a standing desk. Maybe you need your boss to know why you don't check e-mail as frequently as others, because you are setting aside blocks of time to focus. Whatever the reason, it's important to give a brief explanation of your ADHD and the specific symptoms that trip you up at work. Don't go off on tangents about what school was like as a kid or how ADHD is making a mess of your marriage. Stay on topic and be concise.

Here's an example of how a clear and effective conversation might go:

"Hi, Ted. I just want to take a moment and let you know about something that affects my working style. I have ADHD, as do millions of adults. It specifically trips me up at work around achieving good focus. I tend to get distracted by noise and interruptions. The way I plan to address this is to wear noise-canceling headphones when I'm at my desk and limit the frequency of checking e-mail. These two things help me get in the zone and really get a lot done. Are you okay with my doing these two things? Also, do you have any questions or suggestions about my ADHD?"

Bear in mind the specifics of your workplace, the local laws, and your particular situation; use your own discretion when deciding to talk about your ADHD at work.

Next up: Seeing things from another's perspective, looking at problems with a flexible approach to possible solutions, and practicing shifting gears.

Takeaways

- Keeping your environment free of clutter and other messes helps you focus.
- Planning your work helps you avoid distractions.
- Knowing what kind of procrastinator you are lets you watch out for it.
- Using a timer helps you get started and take necessary breaks.
- Prioritizing tasks before starting work ensures you will get important things done.
- Keep your digital device use in check.
- Use a notebook for your to-do list so tasks won't get dropped.
- Your daily to-do list is your friend and should be rewritten and prioritized daily.

4 Strengthen Your Mental Flexibility

Overview

In any book of this nature, terms that sound like technical jargon are inevitable. For example, if I had a room of 100 people at a workshop and asked them to raise their hands if they knew with certainty what cognitive flexibility is, I suspect only about 25 would stick their hands up with confidence. Now, if I asked that same group to take a couple of minutes to define *cognitive* and then a couple of minutes to define *flexibility*, and asked the question again, the number would go up to about 75. Why do I believe this? It's because, as a therapist, I know that a lack of cognitive flexibility can get in the way of figuring out routine problems. *Cognitive flexibility* (CF) is just a fancy term for flexible thinking, with *cognition* meaning "thoughts" or "thinking." CF is the ability to shift from old ideas to new ones, to switch from one task to another, or even to think about two ideas or concepts at the same time. When I, the expert, ask a room full of people a question like, "What is cognitive flexibility?" they get hit with all three requirements for CF. They shift from listening and note-taking to answering (task switching); they may get stuck on an old idea that the word *cognitive* is fancy jargon they don't understand (shifting from an old idea to a new idea); and finally, they may struggle to think about and define the terms *cognitive* and *flexibility* at the same time (thinking about two ideas at once). However, when we slow the thinking process, break it down, and allow for freedom of thought, people can fairly easily come to a pretty clear understanding of cognitive flexibility.

So, what does this have to do with adults with ADHD? Cognitive flexibility is a struggle for a significant subset of people with ADHD. Your head might be nodding as you read this. *Task switching, ouch! That's hard for me. Paying attention to multiple concepts at once? Yes, that's a big deal!*

Neither of these mental capacities is particularly foreign, but they affect how well we function across a huge variety of tasks. However, it's the first component of cognitive flexibility—the bit about abandoning old information or ideas for new things that present themselves—that trips people up the most. As a skill, it's not as familiar as something like task switching, but it's a big deal, especially in the workplace.

The biggest difficulty for adults with ADHD who struggle with CF is mentally switching tracks as quickly and as fluidly as complex tasks often require. This is compounded if there are strong feelings and emotions related to the task or idea. Take this example: John is working from home. He's been grinding away, has found some pretty good focus, and is pushing toward a deadline. His roommate returns home from work and says, "John, you want to grab some dinner?" But John doesn't answer. After all, he's focused, and it can be pretty darn hard to get focused in the first place. His roommate walks a little closer to John's desk and asks again, "*Dude*, you want to get dinner or *what*?" John snaps back, "I'm working!" This example shows how a lack of CF causes a glitch in functioning. For John, switching from working on his project to talking to his roommate is hard, and holding on to the idea he's working on *and* processing his roommate's request is too much for his core skills to manage. The demands of the moment overwhelm him, and he responds with irritation. You can see how this type of interaction could balloon into a big issue in the office. To be fair, no one with ADHD likes to have his or her focus messed with.

So how flexible are you? There are numerous ways to assess your CF. Probably the easiest and most entertaining is the Stroop Effect Test. For over a decade, I gave this test to lecture halls full of college students all at once. The results were typically hilarious. Try it. Look at the words in the illustration and say out loud the color of the text for each word as fast as you can. Ready? *Go!*

red **blue** orange **purple**

orange **blue** green **red**

blue **purple** **green** **red**

orange **blue** red green

purple orange **red** **blue**

green **red** **blue** purple

I expect that when you hit that third line, things went sideways. Some readers will likely be able to catch it after a couple of words and finish it out, but many will continue to struggle. This can give you a glimpse into how your CF is working. To take your self-assessment further, reflect on your experience around task switching, and new versus old ideas, and you will get a better sense of your experience with CF.

EXERCISE **PRACTICING IMPROVISING**

1 First, find a mirror. It can be on a wall, in your hand, or the selfie video function on your phone.

2 Make the face of a particular emotion, such as happiness, but name a different emotion. For example, look in the mirror, smile, and say, "I am angry," or "I am sad."

You might find that your gears grind at first, but you'll get better at it. When we cover problem-solving and perspective taking later, you'll learn even more about how to strengthen your CF.

Flexible Problem-Solving

Oh boy, this is an important one. For more than a decade, I've worked with some of Silicon Valley's brightest minds and biggest names, helping high-level professionals improve their performance even more. My work in both ADHD and executive coaching has landed me smack at the intersection of problem-solving and performance in some of the most demanding professions in the world. Many times I've helped tech leaders bring products to market from behind the scenes. Now, I'm not taking credit for their innovations by any stretch! But I will happily take credit for helping these innovators break the mold and solve some mind-bending problems by improving their mental flexibility. Believe it or not, many of the top executives I've worked with struggle with some ADHD symptoms, which makes sense if you think about ADHD in terms of both its strengths and weaknesses. What I tend to see is that many people with ADHD excel at something called *lateral thinking*, which is the ability to connect divergent ideas that most people would not link. The Silicon Valley movers and shakers who have come to me and overcome hurdles in their work have typically done so because I've pushed them to be highly flexible and, thus, highly creative problem solvers. In fact, some of the biggest breakthroughs have come while they were looking 180 degrees in the other direction from their current path.

Those people are not the ones this chapter is aimed at. This chapter is for people still struggling with CF, not people who've already got a handle on it. The prototypical case I see is someone banging their head (metaphorically) against a wall, trying to solve a new problem by using tiny iterations of a past failed or flawed idea over and over.

Here are some examples:

1   Trying to get a child to leave the playground by saying, "It's time to go," then "Come on, it's time to go," then "We need to go now," then "Come, now, please. We need to head home," when the solution is to say, "We can stay as long as you want today. We just won't be able to come back until next week."

2   Trying to get an employee to come in on time by saying, "We really need you here on time," then "The team wants you here on time for the meetings," then "You are very important to the team, so please be on time," when the solution is to say, "I see that you don't arrive on time for the meetings. The team has decided you are not integral to the meetings, so we will start them without you going forward."

To overcome this stuck thinking, I have clients start to brainstorm ideas about alternative solutions. Ninety percent of the time, the person who is stuck will either shut down an idea before even saying it out loud or discredit it immediately. This type of strategy is about as inflexible as it gets. The good news is that when I temporarily operate as a surrogate for their mental skills, encouraging the easy flow of new ideas, they are able to free up their thinking and land on creative solutions. One way I help people achieve this is to encourage them to embrace absurdity. Yes, you heard that right—absurdity. For example, I'll have them do a thought experiment where they come up with ideas that don't conform to the laws of physics, are not bound by financial constraints, or maybe even use full-on magical thinking. Obviously, these are not the solutions they end up going with, but the exercise frees up their ability to find new solutions.

EXERCISE WHAT'S YOUR ANGLE?

When I hear the question, "What's your angle?" I picture a couple of salespeople scheming about how they're going to make a deal, or maybe a marketing person deciding on a way to present a product to customers. These are actually very helpful images. Why? Because in both cases, people are trying to solve a problem by exploring all the options and deciding which one will be the most successful. All situations have multiple angles or approaches that can lead to varying outcomes.

My friend John K. Coyle is a leader in designing ways of thinking about and solving problems. He ultimately used flexible and creative thinking to win an Olympic medal in speed skating! John has an incredible exercise he uses that very quickly helps people uncover new angles and options.

The entire exercise exists inside one question: What would [blank] do? You can insert the name of many different well-known people, depending on whom you admire. You might choose Steve Jobs, Oprah Winfrey, Stephen Hawking, or an everyday person you admire, like your best friend or a coworker. By temporarily stepping into someone else's shoes, and mind-set, you get yourself out of the way so you can unlock new angles. Give it a try.

1 Answer this question: "How many ways can I walk up the stairs?" You might say, "One step at a time," or, "With my feet."

2 Now ask yourself, "What would a competitive skate-boarder do?" or, "How would a gymnast answer this?"

I think you're going to be pleasantly surprised at just how flexible your thinking can be with a little help from an exercise like this one.

EXERCISE WHAT CAN YOU DO WITH A CARDBOARD BOX?

1 Take your notebook and number 10 lines.

2 Set a timer for two minutes.

3 Until the timer goes off, write down as many uses for a box as you can come up with.

tip **Revisiting childhood.** If you're feeling stuck, transport yourself back to childhood and ask the question again. Children are amazing. They're not yet bound by the rigid rules of adult life and society and all the conventional thinking this implies. Can you make a rocket or a car with a cardboard box? Sure you can, but what else can you make? Remember to harness the power of absurdity and let your imagination run wild. Another productive way to engage in this exercise is to make it concrete: Go find a cardboard box, sit down on the ground with it, and let your mind go.

Perspective Taking

At the beginning of this chapter, I explained that one of the key functions of cognitive flexibility is the ability to hold two different ideas in your mind at once. This can be challenging for a person with ADHD, due to their mind's tendency to land on or stick to the most emotionally charged idea. Even ideas or perspectives that are not emotionally charged can suddenly become so when the perspective is challenged by another person or by evidence showing that the perspective may be mistaken. For example, maybe you believe the world is flat, and someone says, "No, it's not flat; science has proved that. Why do you believe it's flat?" The dynamic of being asked "why" sets off a knee-jerk reaction to defend your position, which can attach you even more firmly to your original idea. In addition, the direct challenge to your belief can trigger enough of an emotional reaction to start pulling the prefrontal cortex (PFC, which you will recall from chapter 1 is the brain's command center for core mental skills) offline. We will cover the role of emotions in ADHD symptoms in the next chapter. For now, just know that when the emotional center for the brain becomes excited and starts taking over, the ability to be flexible, creative, and calm starts to slip away.

Another reason why seeing another person's perspective can be especially hard for adults with ADHD has to do with their brain's "traffic cop" getting sleepy. A traffic cop is the police officer who stands in the middle of an intersection directing traffic when a traffic light is not working. If the officer is not paying attention, the cars coming in multiple directions will crash. The "traffic cop" in the brain directs traffic between information coming into our awareness (sights, sounds) or information coming from within (thoughts, emotions) and information going out (reactions, behaviors, new thoughts). Unfortunately, this sleepy traffic officer gets even sleepier when challenged or bored. For example, maybe your spouse tells you it's a pain in the neck when you leave your documents and work materials all over the kitchen table. This will likely lead to a struggle in seeing her or his perspective. "Huh? What? I like to work in the kitchen by the window!" Sound familiar? If the sleepy traffic cop was on their game, they would pause to evaluate the full picture. In that pause, you have options. You could put yourself in your spouse's shoes, think of a creative solution, or even just ask questions that may bring you to a place of resolution rather than a nose-dive into an argument.

Putting yourself in someone else's shoes is code for *empathy*. Empathy is simply understanding and acknowledging at some level another person's perspective or experience. People with ADHD can be very empathetic and very sensitive to the needs or others. However, perspective taking and empathy can get derailed by the neurological underpinnings of ADHD and other attention-related issues.

EXERCISE SOMEONE ELSE'S SHOES

Let's see what the important skill of perspective taking looks like in action. Many years ago, I was an administrator at a psychiatric facility for children and teens. One year, we got a new kid, about 10 years old and nervous as hell about being there. One way this showed up was his wetting the bed at night. We've all done this at some point as kids; it's not fun, and it's pretty embarrassing. This 10-year-old's roommate was a few years older and took it upon himself to try to shame the boy into stopping the bed wetting. Obviously, this didn't work—shaming only serves to increase anxiety, which was this kid's problem in the first place. I got wind of the prob-lem quickly and met with the older boy. He told me he was trying to help the younger boy stop bed wetting. I tried to reason with him and got absolutely nowhere. In fact, I sat in a conversational power struggle with this kid for so long that I started to wonder if *I* was the one who had problems with cognitive flexibility. So I tried something completely different. I acknowledged that it was probably hard to have his room smell like pee and that he might even feel embarrassed that he had not only a younger roommate but also one who struggled with bed wetting. Once I had his attention and we were no longer in a struggle, I said, "Hey, big guy, imagine this. You come to a new place after experiencing some really tough times, and you start peeing your bed. Your new roommate, who's older, cool, and knows the ropes, starts to make fun of you. How would you feel?" He lifted his eyes and smiled as the lightbulb went on in his head and heart. We were then able to problem-solve in about five minutes, and the issue was gone in two days (and two pee-soaked nights—but solved nonetheless!).

This interaction only worked because I was able to empathize with the older kid's perspective first and then help him get into the younger kid's shoes (perspective) and empathize. It was a perspective-taking twofer, and it worked like magic.

How can you use this strategy to solve your real-life problems? It's simple. The next time a coworker, a friend, your partner, or your child tells you they're frustrated or upset with you about something you've done, *pause*. Before you automatically respond defensively, use the pause to ask yourself what it would be like if that very thing they're complaining about happened to you. Keep in mind that acknowledging and empathizing with someone's perspective doesn't necessarily mean they're right and you're wrong. In fact, their perspective may be downright crazy. But either way, using your mental flexibility to better understand their position will get you to a resolution faster, and with less conflict.

tip **Pausing to gain perspective.** When you find yourself automatically defending your belief, action, or comment, use it as a cue to pause and ask questions about the other person's perspective. More information leads to a more complete understanding of the other person's view.

What's Your Plan B?

Everyone needs a backup plan most of the time. Whenever I give a workshop or lecture, I always have options up my sleeve that will allow me to shift if things go sideways or the conversation takes an unexpected turn. Maybe my content is not resonating after lunch when people are sleepy, or maybe I accidentally stumble onto a topic that's a hot-button issue. Whatever the case, in order to perform well as a presenter and trainer under those circumstances, I need to be able to shift gears quickly, before heads start hitting desks or attendees get too emotionally charged to absorb what I'm saying.

Let's be realistic. In most day-to-day situations, you won't have a backup plan predetermined and ready to go. It can be hard to plan ahead of time, especially with ADHD. So, we need to practice shifting gears and getting to a plan B scenario quickly.

EXERCISE FINDING YOUR PLAN B

Here are two different examples of situations that go wrong. You must be the master plan B maker. In order to achieve this status in the exercise, you need to come up with a plan B for each situation in under 20 seconds. Get out your notebook to jot the plan Bs down, if you wish. You've got this—let's go!

1   Lin is running outside to call a cab for an important interview. She takes the elevator down from the fortieth floor, gets to the lobby, and realizes she forgot her phone upstairs, along with her ID badge. At first, she thinks there's no time to go back up, especially without her badge, and no way to call a cab without her phone. Or is there? How could she secure a cab another way? You have 20 seconds. Go!

2   Your seven-year-old son has a friend over for dinner after a playdate. You're making a spinach, apple, tomato, walnut, and cheese salad when your son says, "Dad, my friend doesn't eat green veggies." Can you adapt the dish you're making? You have 20 seconds. Go!

EXERCISE UNSTICK YOUR MIND

Logic puzzles are another way to sharpen problem-solving. Try to do each of these in 20 seconds or under. Don't forget to set your timer!

1   All grizzly bears have two eyes. Grizzly bears like to eat fish. Fish also have two eyes. One grizzly bear stands in a barn after eating two fish. How many eyes are in the barn?

2   Roses are red, violets are blue: You have one can of red paint and one of blue. You want to paint the fence right

now, but your spouse doesn't like red or blue. What do you do?

tip **Remember to calm your mind in order to see other perspectives.** Pause, breathe deeply, and give yourself time to step outside the box.

Thinking about Thinking

Until we're teenagers, we don't really have the ability to think about our own thinking process—a process psychologists and neurologists call *metacognition*. Metacognition is simply being able to observe, understand, and evaluate our thoughts. Yes, it's thinking about thinking or knowing about knowing, which sounds a little abstract. But fundamentally, it's simply the awareness of our thoughts, the content of those thoughts, what impact they may have on our experience, and how we came to think the thoughts in the first place. We can't change anything in life without awareness. Let's look at an example.

Maybe you believe that all elephants have tusks. I can ask how you came to believe that, and you could tell me. Maybe your parents told you when you were little, or maybe every photo you've ever seen of elephants shows them with tusks. Now, imagine that I come on strong and tell you that I think you are ignorant for your belief. I show you photos from scientific texts or videos online, basically making it nearly impossible for you to argue your point. You get upset and start shouting at me that all elephants have tusks and that I'm being a jerk for insisting otherwise. Then I step back and ask why you are so upset. If you can tell me what you are thinking and what you are feeling in relation to your thoughts, then you're able to zoom out and exercise metacognition. However, if you tell me you don't know, that "it's just the way it is," and you can't tell me more about what you are thinking and why, you are not exercising metacognition and won't be able to mount any defense for your argument.

Let's look at another example. My daughter is five years old. She often gets upset about some situation involving a friend or classmate. She might say, "Daddy, I'm so mad at Alma! Look what she did! She tore my drawing!" Being an adult with a fully developed brain, I might say, "Oh sweetie, I see that. I'm so sorry. Why do you think she did that?" I prompt her to reconstruct her thoughts about the event, because in order for her to use metacognition to understand her own thoughts or the thoughts and motives of others, my daughter would need to be a bit older developmentally. Because she is five, she will likely say, "I don't know why she did it; she just did it!" Upon further exploration, it turns out that Alma saw the drawing and picked it up to look at it, and my daughter freaked out and snatched it back, causing the drawing to tear. In this example, it took my using my adult brain to methodically sift through the events to help her understand what actually happened. Was my daughter being evasive to avoid taking responsibility for her own mistake? Maybe—she is pretty savvy that way—but not likely. She was essentially stuck, because her brain had not developed to the point of providing her the ability to engage her core mental skills. She wasn't able to use metacognition to think about her thoughts or to try to imagine Alma's possible thoughts or motives.

GRADE YOUR OWN HOMEWORK

Below is a brief writing prompt. I want you to spend however long you need to write half a page on the topic. This is not a grammar exam. You don't need to proof it or spend very long on it—half an hour max will probably do. When you're done, there will be a series of questions for you to answer about it. Note: *Do not* read the questions first.

Writing prompt: In about half a page (typed or handwritten) explain three of the biggest struggles that adults with ADHD face on a daily basis. Please write it in narrative format, not just a list of symptoms. Please explain the struggles as if the person reading your response knows nothing about what you are talking about. When you are done, turn the page and ask yourself the follow-up questions.

1 Why did you choose those three struggles?

2 Are those struggles shared by most people with ADHD or just you?

3 How did you feel when writing the examples? Were they difficult to come up with?

4 Do you think your examples were clearly explained?

By answering these questions, you will have flexed your metacognition mental muscles.

tip **In order to use metacognition, you need to take a brief pause.** Try to decide on a few key areas in your life where you need to use metacognition in order to help improve your functioning and quality of life. By doing so, you will be more likely to be aware in the moment and pause in order to think about your thinking (metacognition).

SELF-MONITORING

Using metacognition to monitor your thinking is key to managing your emotions. For example, imagine that you just waited 10 minutes for a parking spot, only to have someone sneak their car in front of you and take it. You might feel so angry that you want to scream curse words out the window, but you check yourself and decide to look for another spot, rather than embarrass yourself.

You experience difficult or strong emotions, just as we all do. Being able to have some control over how intense the emotions are and the effect they have on your behavior is critical to your success. You need awareness of your emotions and the thoughts behind them in order to manage them. In the next chapter, we will look more closely at emotions and techniques for managing them. In preparation for that, and to further hone cognitive flexibility, let's try the following self-monitoring exercise.

While following the steps below, be aware of what you are thinking and feeling as you go along:

1 Take out a piece of paper.

2 Take out a pen or pencil.

3 Fold the piece of paper in half.

4 Count from 1 to 10 in your mind or out loud.

5 Write down the numbers 11 to 20 on either side of the folded paper.

6 Unfold the paper.

7 Count from 1 to 10 again in your mind or out loud.

8 Fold the paper again, the same way it was before.

9 Write down the numbers 11 to 20 again on either side of the folded paper.

10 Unfold the paper again.

11 Place the paper on the table for three minutes.

12 Put the paper in the recycling bin and go about your day.

13 Say to yourself in your mind or out loud what you thought and felt as you went through the exercise.

Note: Yes, I understand that this exercise probably left you frustrated or annoyed. That was the goal. People with ADHD tend to hate steps, especially those that seem pointless (or are, in fact, pointless). *But*, did you notice your thoughts and feelings while doing it? Could you tell how they were affecting your performance? Did you make it through all 13 steps? If not, do you know why not?

Changing Gears

Anyone reading this book likely has a laundry list of ways in which ADHD makes life hard. Maybe you have even more than a laundry list—some of you could probably write a PhD dissertation or an encyclopedia volume on the headaches that come with ADHD. That said, there is one thorn in the side of everyone with ADHD: changing gears. Changing gears may come in the form of transitioning from one task or activity to another, moving from one location to another, interruptions to work flow, and so on. Most adults with ADHD also feel that they are either completely stuck in one gear or all the way on the other end of the spectrum, slipping from one gear to the next with almost no control. It doesn't matter on which end of the continuum you find yourself: Both can wreak havoc on efficiency and quality of life.

Let's look at an example of being on time. Jorge and Beatrice live in different countries and have different jobs, and both have ADHD. They both need to be at work at 9:00 a.m., and both are often 45 minutes late to work. They both have a boss who has finally lost patience and calls them in to discuss the issue. "Why are you late again? What's going on? Why do you have so much trouble getting here on time?!" I bet just reading those words from a pretend boss gives you an elevated heart rate, triggers shame, and makes you want to run and hide. I don't blame you. I felt that way just writing it. If I could play a tape of Jorge and Beatrice each answering the "why?" question, it would probably sound like an echo, because they'd be saying the same things—maybe in a different order and with different emphasis, but their answers would probably revolve around the central problem of being unable to *switch gears* from one task to another or from one goal to another. You might hear, "I'm sorry. I'm so sorry. I just get caught up, and time slips away. Yesterday I tried to do 15 things before leaving the apartment to come here. Today I got stuck trying to finish something and couldn't stop, even though I knew I needed to. I feel ridiculous. It won't happen again."

"It won't happen again." How many times have we said that, just to see it happen again hours or days later. Telling others that it won't happen again without a plan to ensure success is just a setup for disappointment. In the following exercises, we will look at some ways to get better at mindful intention—a strategy for supporting your important "gear-switching" function that we discussed in chapter 2. In the digital/Internet age, we're constantly being interrupted and called on to shift gears from what's in front of us to a news alert, text from a friend, or cute kitty video. This is a challenge for everyone, but people with ADHD can get totally derailed by even minor interruptions. Mindful intention is a powerful antidote to digital (and other) distractions. When we use mindful intention, we're deciding in the moment what we want or need to do, and acting on it with purpose. Falling into a rabbit hole of social media is usually anything but intentional—unless you're purposefully taking a break. Pausing and mindfully taking time to zone out surfing the web is okay, as long as you don't do it so often it gets in the way of your success.

Several skills need to be used together in order to get gradually better at effectively shifting gears. Think about what a person who's shifting gears has to do. She needs to be able to pause, become aware of her task demands, use self-monitoring, and, finally, shift her attention. ADHD makes all parts of attentional shifting harder, which makes practicing this much more important. Attentional shifting can be a powerful tool when used correctly. It's not a quick fix or magic bullet, but it is a set of skills that build on each other.

Attention is interesting in that everyone (with ADHD or not) tends to pay attention to the things we tend to pay attention to. This isn't a tongue twister or a riddle. It's the same idea that's at play in the law of physics that states "what's in motion stays in motion." Have you ever met someone who seems to always focus on the negative? You may have a friend or coworker who always points out what's wrong or what could be better. Those people are often a drain to be around. You say what a beautiful day it is, and they respond with, "Yeah, but it's too windy"; or you mention that you love to swim in the ocean, and they counter with statistics about shark attacks. These people have spent so much time focusing on the negative that their attention now automatically shifts to the negative. *Things in motion stay in motion.*

Using the power of attentional shift to create positive change in your life is surprisingly simple. But simple is not the same thing as easy. Changing what your attention lands on in an almost automatic way takes time and effort, but it certainly is not complicated. The process is the inverse of what we just saw in the example of the person who always focuses on the negative. Using this principle to improve the focus/attention symptoms of your ADHD is about focusing on the right things at the right times. If you need to focus daily on getting your kids dressed for school at 7:00 a.m., you don't want your attention to shift to work, what you want for breakfast, or a cute Instagram post. You want to keep your attention squarely on getting the kids ready, regardless of what distractions arise. This also applies to beliefs you hold about yourself and the world, and it can have a profound influence on motivation. If you only focus on all the times you've struggled with certain activities, you are not likely to be motivated to engage in those activities. It's a lot like skiing or driving in that we tend to go in the direction we are looking.

EXERCISE HARNESSING ATTENTIONAL SHIFT

You can't address all of your attention struggles at once, so let's start by trying to change just one. That said, let's make sure the thing we target has broad, far-reaching implications.

What is one area of focus that you want to change? An easy way to identify your target is to reflect on the people, tasks, or situations about which you regularly have a negative internal dialogue. In other words, what do you beat yourself up about? That's usually a good clue that it's something you really want to change. For example, "Oh, there's Sean. He's going to make me feel bad for not having my weekly report on time *again*. I'll go hide in the break room." Or, "The person in the cube next to me is clearing his throat for the hundredth time this morning. I can't think straight!" Or, "There's my video game console; I can't wait to play it later. Maybe just one game before work will be okay."

1 Choose one negative thing that consistently pulls your attention.

2 Write that negative thing down on a sticky note and place it on your bathroom mirror.

3 On a separate sticky note, write down where you want your attention to be instead, when encountering what you wrote in step 2.

4 Every day for seven days, read out loud the name or description of the negative attention–grabbing thing in step 2. Then read out loud the name or description of the positive thing you wrote in step 3.

5 Repeat this process every seven days with a different negative attention–grabbing thing. Over time, you will develop better awareness of where your attention is landing and gain some control over it.

tip **Practice changing your work environment.** You might find that a different location or environment, even as small as changing the location of your desk or cube, can help jump-start a change in attentional shift.

EXERCISE SELF-INTERRUPTION

Interruptions happen; there's no denying that. Often, the most abundant and unrecognized interruptions are our own.

1   Keep your notebook with you for three days, for as much of the day as possible.

2   Choose one empty page to use for tracking. Every time you get off task or are interrupted, make a mark in the book. Put a small *X* every time you interrupt your own focus, and put a small *O* every time someone or something external interrupts you.

This will heighten your awareness of how often you interrupt yourself. Keep in mind that self-interruptions can be thoughts, websites, text messages, doodles, projects, cleaning, grooming, petting the dog, and so on. Anything you initiate, whether an activity or thought that takes you off task, counts.

> **tip** **Inventory your emotions.** Distractions based in fear, sadness, or any negative emotion are often the hardest to resist. Whenever you feel distracted, take a pause to do an internal inventory of what emotions are showing up for you in that moment. Do you feel anxious? Sad? Angry? Simple awareness of the source of our distraction can help get us back on track.

You have now learned how to be more flexible in your thinking and the value it can bring to your life. In the next chapter, we will look at the role intense emotions can play in your performance and how to develop skills for managing them.

Takeaways

- Cognitive flexibility is the ability to shift from one task to another, move from an old idea to a new one, or hold more than one idea or concept in your head at the same time.
- Mentally switching tracks is harder if there are strong feelings attached to the task or idea.
- Pausing before reacting creates space for options.
- Developing empathy and learning to see a situation or belief from someone else's perspective leads to faster problem resolution with less conflict.
- Practice developing a plan B for when things take an unexpected turn to improve your ability to shift gears.
- Metacognition is the ability to observe, understand, and evaluate our thoughts, which is important for self-regulation.

5 Enhance Your Emotion Regulation

Overview

Everyone experiences difficult emotions like anger, sadness, frustration, or anxiety. However, people with ADHD tend to have a significantly harder time managing the intensity of their emotions. It can often feel as though emotions are happening without your consent or control.

You might have heard or read the term *emotion regulation* in self-help articles and books. Emotion regulation is the act of identifying the feelings you are experiencing and making a conscious effort to control the intensity of those feelings.

When I talk to adult clients about emotional regulation, 99 percent of the time, we are talking about negative emotions. Everyone experiences negative emotions, such as fear, more intensely than positive ones, like contentment. If fear were not such a strong emotion, early humans would not have survived as a species. Thousands of years ago, we needed to be afraid of a predator attacking us. There were no labels on the berries we picked, so we needed to remember which berries made people sick and to fear those berries. Unfortunately, in today's world, negative emotions can be misplaced, and for adults with ADHD, these emotions can get out of control like a wildfire.

Uncontrolled intense emotions can make it hard to think clearly, or lead you to make impulsive choices or to be unnecessarily hard on yourself and others. Life is naturally full of emotional ups and downs, and you must be able to limit how high the highs get and how low the lows go; otherwise life becomes a nasty roller-coaster ride. Years back, I coined the term "emotional electric fence" as a metaphor for the experience adults with ADHD have when they get stuck in an intense negative emotion. We've all seen the old cartoons of a character grabbing an electric fence and being unable to let go. The intense direct electrical current freezes the muscles and prevents them from breaking free. Negative emotions work the same way, by causing the brain to freeze or get stuck on the negative emotion, which leads to a host of relational, occupational, or personal problems. An example of this is getting extremely angry when someone moves or misplaces something you need at home, which leads you to shout or say hurtful things. Another example is turning that anger inward when you misplace something, which causes you to say hurtful things to yourself that lead to lowered self-esteem. This same process often happens when you are anxious about getting a project done on time, which leads you to procrastinate or feel frozen when trying to start.

Emotions don't live in the same part of the brain as your ability to control them. Think about emotions as the gas pedal in a race car that is located in the middle of your brain. The middle of your brain (limbic system) is not where ADHD symptoms live. ADHD is predominantly caused by deficits in the front of the brain (prefrontal cortex), where your core functions live. The brakes for this emotional race car are part of your core functions. So, when you step on the gas and rev up the engine of intense emotions, you may find that the brake pedal isn't strong enough to slow the emotional race car.

In this chapter, you will improve your awareness of your feelings, where they are coming from, and how they are connected to your body. You will also learn skills for managing them when they arise and ultimately become more resilient in the face of negative emotions and overwhelm.

How Are You Feeling?

If you have been following along since the beginning of the book, you can probably guess what I'm going to say next. Yes, that's right: awareness! Nothing can change without it. You might have spent your whole life feeling that emotions come out of nowhere, and before you know it, they are getting in the way of your success. You might have experienced the cascade of negative emotions and negative self-talk that follows a mistake such as being late, forgetting an appointment, or getting distracted. In order to control these emotions, you need to be able to name them as they are happening. Unfortunately, society does a pretty bad job of helping people understand their emotions. Although that's improving, the message most men get is that they can be angry or happy—that's it. Women are given the message that they can have every emotion except anger. Both of these restrictions are truly ridiculous. All people experience all emotions to varying degrees. These gender-based emotional scripts or societal rules keep people from achieving full awareness of their feelings.

Reflect on your own experience for a moment. Think about the emotions you experience the most. When I ask adults to do this in my office, they often give me a list of thoughts like, "I'm terrible at getting things done," or "Everyone thinks I don't care about my job, because I'm late a lot." Those are thoughts that lead to feelings, but they are not actual feelings. Emotions or feelings typically are one word long. Now, think about it again, but use single feeling words like *sad*, *happy*, *angry*, *excited*, *proud*, *worried*, and so on. Below is a list of common feelings to help you.

COMMON EMOTIONS AND FEELINGS

Joyful	Nervous	Defeated
Angry	Helpless	Powerless
Bored	Content	Dread
Rejected	Proud	Bitter
Satisfied	Excited	Confused
Amused	Shocked	Overwhelmed
Helpless	Uncomfortable	Optimistic
Guilty	Restless	Hurt
Regretful	Lonely	Calm
Exhausted	Relaxed	Depressed
Insecure	Relieved	Hopeful
Sad	Confident	Eager
Happy	Anxious	Scared
Annoyed	Humiliated	Ashamed

Did you notice anything interesting? Which of these emotions do you experience most often?

One of the most common negative emotions for everyone with ADHD is shame. Shame is an overarching emotion that starts in childhood and can become a roadblock to success in adulthood. Shame tends to lead to avoidance, diminished confidence, increased distraction, and a whole host of problems that just lead to more shame.

One of the most common positive emotions for people with ADHD is excitement. Getting excited about a new idea, hobby, job, or new relationship feels great! When excitement leads to accomplishment, it feels even better. Unfortunately, when excitement is followed by lack of follow-through on an idea, a hobby falling by the wayside, struggles at work, or a relationship crashing and burning, the resulting emotion is typically negative.

There you have it: the emotional roller-coaster ride of ADHD.

Let's do some exercises to help you build awareness of your emotions.

WRITING PROMPT IDENTIFYING EMOTIONS

Either in your notebook or using your computer, write down your responses to the following three scenarios. You will be labeling the emotions that the person in each scenario is likely experiencing. Labeling emotions in other people can be easier than labeling them for yourself at first. You can refer to the list of common emotions and feelings on page 94.

SCENARIO 1 *Elisa stays up late working on a report that she procrastinated on. She will present it at work the next day for her whole team.*

- What is Elisa likely feeling as she works late into the night to meet the deadline?

Elisa gets to the meeting on time and sets up her presentation. As her team is filing into the conference room, she realizes that she prepared the wrong report. She prepared a report for a project that ended weeks ago.

- What is Elisa likely feeling as she stands in front of her team empty-handed?

SCENARIO 2 *Lee is headed to a fancy restaurant for a first date with someone he's had a crush on for a long time.*

- On the way to the date, what is Lee likely feeling?

Lee arrives right on time and finds his date there waiting for him with a big smile and hug. They enjoy a wonderful meal with plenty of fun conversation and flirtation. They walk out together, and his date turns to him and says, "I had a really nice time. When can we see each other again?"

- What is Lee likely feeling after a great date and being invited for a second date?

SCENARIO 3 *DeShawn and his best friend, Luis, won front-row tickets to see their favorite band play. While waiting for the show to start, someone spills a full drink all over both of them. DeShawn and Luis are soaked with sticky soda. DeShawn has ADHD, and Luis does not. Both of them are shocked. Luis turns to DeShawn and says, "No big deal, man—show's about to start. Let's go up front!" DeShawn tells Luis he will be right back and stomps off to the restroom to try to dry off.*

- What is DeShawn likely feeling as he is walking to the restroom, soaked in soda?

DeShawn is almost totally dry in the restroom. Then he hears the band start playing. He begins to rush and bangs the funny bone in his elbow on the corner of the sink.

- What are all the different emotions that DeShawn likely experiences during this time in the restroom? Remember, he enters feeling one way, probably starts feeling a different way as things improve, then feels differently as he bangs his elbow.

SITTING WITH EMOTIONS

Sometimes the best thing you can do when experiencing diffi-cult emotions is to sit and experience the emotion, rather than try to make them go away or become upset that you are expe-riencing them. When you layer on more negative emotions out of frustration or you do something impulsive to try to feel better, you just create more problems. Instead of one problem, now you have two or three.

When you sit with an emotion, you are simply labeling it, allowing yourself to feel it without trying to control it. I remember experiencing a lot of anxiety when my wife and I were deciding whether to have a second child. I reached out to my mentor to discuss it. He asked what I was worried about. I told him I was worried that two kids would be harder on our careers, lifestyle, and relationship. He looked at me and said, "Yes. It will be all of those things." Instead of his response making me freak out with anxiety, it led me to sit with my feelings, and in a matter of moments, I felt better. Simply acknowledging and accepting an emotion allows it to run its course, and the intensity of it fades.

1 In your notebook, write down something that is unresolved or bothering you right now. It might be a problem at work, a struggle in a relationship, something going on with family, and so on.

2 Find a comfortable place to sit. Get out your notebook and read out loud the thing that's bothering you.

3 Close your eyes. Visualize the situation and allow a feel-ing to come up. As it does, don't fight it. Simply label it. Is it sadness, frustration, or fear? Make sure to use the words "I feel" and not "I am"; for example, "I feel ner-vous." Remember that feelings happen to you; they are not you.

4 Take slow, full, natural breaths. No need to force the air in or out. Just breathe naturally and fully while continuing to label the feeling. You will notice that the feeling loses its intensity.

Watch your emotions rise and fall. Remember the Isaac Newton quote: "What goes up must come down"? The same is true of your emotions. Remind yourself of this when you experience an intense emotion; then simply observe as the highest intensity of the emotion eventually comes back down to a manageable level. No emotion lasts forever. If they did, you would still be riding high from your first birthday party!

The Mind-Body Connection

Surprisingly, most people are not aware that the mind and body are connected. Of the people who do believe the mind and body are connected, many believe that they are only connected in one direction—meaning they believe the mind controls the body, but the body has no effect on the mind. Knowledge of the mind-body connection and the way our physical feelings affect our mental feelings has been around for thousands of years, yet we still know so little.

The easiest way to understand the connection is to think about the word *hangry*. *Hangry* is a term used to explain when someone is angry and cranky, because they are hungry. Not enough energy is coming into the body through food, which leads to negative emotions. Another example is how people tend to be in a good mood and a bit sleepy after eating a hearty meal. When people are full, the neurochemical serotonin is released. Serotonin regulates mood and sleep along with some other important functions.

So let's agree that the mind and body are connected and learn how you can use this knowledge to change how you feel.

There is so much to learn by listening to your body. You do this already. When you are physically hurt, you pay attention to the pain and act accordingly. You may also notice when you are stressed, because you have a tight neck and shoulder muscles, or maybe an upset stomach. I can already imagine the e-mails showing up in my inbox from angry readers telling me, "You just need to put pain out of your mind and keep going!" or, "Stomachaches are for babies!" Don't get me wrong; stubbing your toe or having indigestion from a spicy lunch is usually no reason to alter how you go about your day. However, if you want to live the best life possible, you need knowledge of pain, and your body can provide you with a wealth of it. You just have to listen.

What you put into your body in the form of food, drinks, or even drugs and alcohol has a profound effect on your emotional well-being and cognitive functioning. How much sleep you get and whether it's consistent has a direct effect on emotional well-being, energy, memory, and focus. Physical exercise or lack of exercise has a profound effect on your stress levels, emotional control, mood, and focus.

Let's look at tips for how you can use sleep, nutrition, and exercise to improve your emotion regulation and other symptoms of ADHD.

Note: Please consult your health care provider before making any changes to diet, exercise, or lifestyle.

Sleep like a baby. If a baby doesn't get enough sleep or its sleep schedule deviates from the norm by just a small amount, there will be tantrums and tears. You are no different. You can tolerate less sleep and less consistency, but only within a reasonable range.

(tip) Your sleep and wake times should be consistent. Decide on a bedtime and make it a consistent target. One hour or more before bedtime, stop looking at screens on smartphones, tablets, or computers. Also stop any work-related activities and give your brain time to wind down. Use an alarm and possibly a timer on your lights in the bedroom to help you wake up at the same time each day. Your mind and body thrive on regularity.

(tip) Fuel yourself with food. Your brain uses about 25 percent of the calories you eat! That ball of nerve tissue between your ears only weighs three pounds but requires one-quarter of your energy. You'd better put the right gas in the tank.

(tip) As with sleep, meal times should be consistent. At a minimum, shoot for three meals a day. Don't skip breakfast! For optimal mood and mental performance, you want to eat within an hour of waking up, and make sure breakfast is high in healthy fats and proteins, and low in refined carbohydrates like flour or sugar. Lunch should be around the same time each day, and so should dinner. In order to avoid an afternoon crash, make sure your lunch is not too heavy but does have good amounts of vitamins and minerals. Green vegetables and whole grains are a great way to get B vitamins, which are important for mental energy. Dinner should be similar to lunch; however, a dinner that includes carbohydrates that are slower to digest, like sweet potatoes, can improve sleep by providing a slow release of serotonin during sleep. Nuts and seeds are great for consistent mental and physical energy. An article published by Harvard Health Publishing found that a lack of seeds and nuts in diets worldwide is a leading cause of health issues.

(tip) You were built to move. Currently, the predominant theory about human physical evolution is that our brains are big so that we can carry out complex movements—and lots of them. The saying "born to run" is not just a cute slogan for T-shirts at marathon races. We also know that exercise raises base levels of certain neurochemicals that are important for focus, attention, and mood. Movement also reduces the buildup of stress hormones that wreak havoc on mood and memory.

Like sleep and nutrition, exercise is best when consistent. You don't need a gym membership or any special equipment. All you need is your body. You can go for a walk, do yoga, do push-ups, run, swim, play with your kids, and even turn chores like vacuuming into exercise if you do them with gusto. What's important is that it happens regularly—preferably daily, even if for only five minutes. If you want the biggest return on your time spent exercising, then elevate your heart rate for 30 to 45 minutes a day while exercising. According to Dr. John Ratey, of Harvard University, exercising at a moderate intensity for 30 minutes five days a week can have profound benefits for your mental well-being, memory, and focus.

Build Your Resilience

Have you ever had your day totally derailed by an intense negative emotion? Have the daily hassles and frustrations from your ADHD made you want to give up trying to improve? Does criticism knock you down and make it hard to bounce back?

If you answered yes to these questions, then you probably need to improve your emotional and cognitive resiliency. Improved resiliency will allow you to keep functioning in the face of major negative events, as well as smaller daily hassles and criticisms.

Emotional resilience is a big deal. The military spends a large amount of time building up physical resilience in soldiers so they can face the extreme physical demands of battle. But all the physical resilience in the world is nearly worthless without emotional resilience, so the military also spends time training the men and women of the armed forces to withstand things like psychological torture and mental exhaustion. The higher up the chain, the more time is spent on mental resilience. For example, the Navy Seals and the Army Special Operations Forces units receive extensive training in emotional resilience and mental stamina, due to the high level of importance and complexity of their missions.

Life is complex, and for people with ADHD, it is more complex and emotionally draining than for the average person. This is in part due to the increased sensitivity to emotions that comes with ADHD. But it's possible to reduce the negative effects that intense emotions and daily frustrations bring. In other words, you can become more resilient.

These are some of the key traits of people with emotional resilience:

- They are able to hear criticism from others and from themselves without melting in self-defeat or burning up in an emotional wildfire.
- They are able to use the support of others to gain strength.
- They have an optimistic view of outcomes while remaining realistic.
- They face their challenges and fears rather than constantly avoiding them.
- They take care of their physical well-being.
- They remain flexible and open to new ideas and perspectives.
- They listen to criticism and use it as information for growth.
- They are persistent in their endeavors when faced with challenges and setbacks.
- They are empathetic to others and their viewpoints.
- They accept that change is part of life, so they work to adapt, rather than fight, all changes.
- They pause and are thoughtful rather than constantly impulsive.

When you read that list, what did you think? What did you feel?

If you read it and only thought about how you don't have all of those traits and are, therefore, a "lost cause," you will need to work a little more to build resilience. If you read it and thought about how you want to develop those traits, you are likely on a better footing to become resilient.

Even if you thought, "I'm a lost cause," there is good news for you. When my clients are initially resistant and seem defeated, it does take extra work to start on the path toward growth. However, once they get going, they tend to stay the course—in many cases doing better than those who don't have to work as hard for it.

EXERCISE WHAT DOES RESILIENCE LOOK LIKE?

The goal of this exercise is to help you begin to see yourself as resilient.

1 Identify three areas of your life where you tend to struggle a lot emotionally. If you can, identify one area that is personal (you bring yourself down with negative self-talk), one that is relational (someone is critical toward you or opposes your perspective), and one that is task based or occupational (at home or at work). Once you have identified three areas, write them in your notebook.

2 Refer to the list of traits of emotionally resilient people (page 102) and identify a few that would be helpful to apply to each of the three areas you listed in step 1.

3 Write down how you will use each of the resiliency traits.

4 Write down a new narrative about yourself as an emotionally resilient person who uses the traits from steps 2 and 3.

- "I am an emotionally resilient person who asks other people at work for their perspectives and thoughtfully decides whether their perspectives are valuable for me to include in my work."
- "I am an emotionally resilient person who reaches out to my best friend for support when I am being hard on myself for my mistakes and shortcomings."
- "I am an emotionally resilient person who goes for long walks every morning so I can have more control over my emotional reactions with my family in the morning."

tip **Do something scary every day.** According to performance and productivity expert Timothy Ferriss, often the thing you need to do most is the thing you are most afraid of. Take that advice and do something every day that scares you. It may be small, like ordering a weird flavor of ice cream, or something big, like calling the CEO of the company you are trying to do business with and pitching a project. You will know what to do, because it's scary or different. Note: You don't need to do anything dangerous or crazy to benefit from this technique.

tip **Be a guide for others.** Now that you are working hard to build your emotional resilience, it's time to spread your wisdom. Look around for people in your life who are struggling and help them use the emotional resilience traits you learned in this section. You will learn by teaching.

Managing Negative Emotions

When you experience intense negative emotions, it can be very helpful to take a break, go for a walk, call a friend or family member for support, or write out your thoughts and feelings in a journal. Unfortunately, you won't always be able to step away from a situation. When you can't, you need something that will allow you to address the intense emotions.

A very effective way is to use a mindfulness and breathing technique I developed to use in my own life. The technique is called the 3x3 Method and has proven to be extremely helpful for thousands of people. You can learn more about the technique and the backstory by watching my TED talk on it (see References, page 142). For now, I'm going to get it into your hands so you can start benefiting from it also.

When you are feeling negative emotions or stress, or you are worrying about the future or the past, you can use the 3x3 Method to immediately get you back on track. The technique is extremely simple and only takes 30 seconds.

1 Identify three physical objects in your environment. They can be anything—your desk, a water bottle, a person, a pen, the wall.

2 Name one of the objects and take one deep breath and exhale. Then repeat with the second object and then the third object. For example, "That's a water bottle (take a deep breath in and then exhale). That's a pen (take a deep breath in and then exhale). That's a chair (take a deep breath in and then exhale)."

And that's it. The technique very quickly turns off your overactive mind by bringing you back to the present, and the deep breaths quickly calm the nervous system. Keep in mind that most people to whom I have taught this looked at me as if I were crazy at first. It seems too simple—until you try it.

EXERCISE THE 48-HOUR REVIEW

The goal of this exercise is to build up your awareness of negative emotions in the moment.

1 In your notebook, create a list of as many negative emotions as you can think of. You can refer to the list of emotions and feelings on page 94.

2 During the next 48 hours, put a small check next to each negative emotion you experience. You may have several checks next to some emotions and none on others.

Note: If you aren't able to do this exercise during the day, you can do it as a review of the day about an hour before you go to bed. It will still give you a good sense of the negative emotions that you experience most.

EXERCISE DO-OVER

The goal of this exercise is to improve the types of interaction you have with others when you're in an emotional state. A great way to practice is to go back and redo an interaction that didn't go well.

1 Think back a few days or weeks and identify a time when you responded emotionally to someone and wish you had done it differently. It can be small, like being curt or snarky with a friend or family member.

2 Go back to that person or call them and redo your response. Maybe your spouse asked you whether you picked up milk, and you snapped, "*Yes!* Give me a break!" In that case, you can say to him or her, "The other day, when you asked me if I bought milk and I snapped at you, I meant to say, 'Yes, I did get milk. Thank you for making sure.'" If you are inclined to apologize also, that's even better.

tip **Take a pause.** Emotional reactions can lead you to blurt out angry responses, so it's important to practice pausing before responding. This pause may be in person or in a text, chat, or e-mail. To practice, simply pause a few minutes before responding to a message.

TALKING WITH FAMILY OR FRIENDS ABOUT ADHD

You likely already know that ADHD can have a negative effect on your relationships. It's likely not news to your family and friends, either. However, they probably don't fully understand what ADHD causes and what it doesn't.

I specialize in treating adults with ADHD, and I have an additional specialty of treating couples where one person has ADHD. I often hear stories about how someone's relationship fell apart largely due to their partner and how their therapist didn't understand ADHD, which led the therapist to misinterpret behaviors as selfish or intentionally malicious. Don't get me wrong: People with ADHD can be as selfish as anyone else, but the wrong things tend to get labeled as selfish. The topic of couples and ADHD is a big one. I offer a popular workshop on the subject and regularly provide training and consultation to other therapists who don't know how to address it in their work with clients. Here, I just want to offer you a basic framework for talking with your family and friends about your ADHD. As with talking with coworkers, you will need to use your personal judgment to decide whether or not to discuss your ADHD with them.

In order to have a productive conversation, you will want to be clear and concise, and to make an extra effort to empathize with the other person's experience of you. Maybe they are frustrated due to your impulsive behaviors, feel that you intentionally leave messes around to upset them, or think that because you get distracted during conversations, you don't care about them. Whatever the case, ADHD symptoms can be hard for both you and those close to you.

When you are talking with friends or family, try to understand exactly the ways in which your ADHD may be a problem in that relationship. Speak to them in a way that feels collaborative and understanding of their frustration, while being direct about how your ADHD contributes to the issue. Be careful not to blame everything on ADHD and come across as helpless. At this point in the book, I hope you have seen that you're not helpless.

Here is an example of how a conversation with a friend or family member might go:

"Hi, Chiara. I'm sorry about being late again. I know it's very frustrating and probably makes you feel like I don't care enough to be on time. That couldn't be further from the truth. I have ADHD, and it trips me up in a number of ways. One of the biggest and most annoying is my struggle with being on time. I am working on it and thought it would be helpful to share a bit about it with you. The reason I end up being late for our dates is because I get stuck trying to make sure I have the right outfit on and everything in place for the date. Believe it or not, I'm actually a perfectionist. I know you probably don't associate ADHD with perfectionism, but it's more common than most people realize. I care so much about our time together and wanting to make a good impression that I get stuck in the details and end up being late. I know it's a total hassle and makes you feel unimportant, and I'm sorry. Maybe we can brainstorm some ways I can communicate with you when I'm running late? You might even have some great ideas that would help me be on time for our dates."

Managing Overwhelm

Everyone in the world experiences overwhelm from time to time. How much overwhelm someone experiences varies greatly depending on personality, work setting, home life, and lifestyle choices. For some people with ADHD, overwhelm can be an almost daily occurrence. Overwhelm can have far-reaching negative impacts on your home life, work life, and relationships. It can lead to procrastination and avoidance, and cause people to shut down or give up trying in certain situations.

Overwhelm tends to happen when tasks are seen as big and unmanageable, or negative emotions run unchecked and become too strong. Another big contributor to overwhelm is uncertainty. People like to know what the outcomes of situations will be ahead of time or how to address new or intimidating situations.

The generic definition of *overwhelm* is "to bury or drown beneath a huge mass." That's certainly a fitting description of how it can feel. Things become too much and the weight feels too heavy to bear.

1   In your notebook, write down 0, 1, or 2 for each question to rate your personal experience. Your answers should reflect what you believe about yourself, not what other people think about you.

0 – No or never
1 – Sometimes
2 – Yes or often

- You don't get a chance to relax or sit down for healthy meals on a daily basis.
- You start each day worrying about everything you need to get done.
- You are very hard on yourself each evening for not getting everything done.
- You are unable to complete your tasks for the day.
- You are overburdened or exhausted.
- You have demands from many areas of your life (work, parenting, spouse, home, friends, family) that seem never ending.
- You get very little to no time for yourself.
- You feel that there is no way out of your situation.
- You think to yourself that you cannot keep going on like this.
- You regularly receive bodily sensations such as your heart beating fast or pounding, headaches, tense muscles, upset stomach, or stomachaches.

2 Add up your answers to get your total score.

- If your total score is below 9, you are likely experiencing a low level of overwhelm.
- If your total score is between 10 and 15, you are experiencing moderate levels of overwhelm.
- If your total score is between 16 and 20, you are experiencing high levels of overwhelm.

EXERCISE BUILDING UNCERTAINTY TOLERANCE

In order to become better at tolerating uncertainty, you must practice being exposed to uncertainty.

1 Identify three situations that you avoided out of discomfort, fear, and so on, and write them down in your notebook. They may be projects, places, or people you have avoided.

2 Sit down in a place where you won't be interrupted.

3 For the first situation, write down all the possible negative outcomes. Note: Only work on one situation at a time until step 6. You can do the exercise for each situation in separate sittings or on different days if you find it more comfortable.

4 For that same first situation, write down all the possible positive outcomes.

5 Notice all the emotions that come up during the exercise for that one situation and write them down.

6 Repeat steps 3 to 5 for the second and third situations.

7 Reflect on your experience. Were you surprised by anything? Did you gain any insights that can help you the next time you avoid something or struggle with something due to uncertainty?

tip **Uncertainty "workouts."** Every time you find yourself avoiding something or feeling anxious about it due to uncertainty, ask yourself what all the possible outcomes may be. Don't shut down any ideas; allow them to come up, no matter how silly, and write them all down. As with lifting weights, the more you work on your ability to brainstorm all outcomes, the stronger you will become at quickly seeing all options in uncertain situations.

EXERCISE IDENTIFY ALTERNATIVE BEHAVIORS

1 Go back to your list of three situations from the previous exercise, "Building Uncertainty Tolerance."

2 For each situation, identify how you behaved when you were avoiding it. Did you procrastinate? Did you give up? Did you do something else instead?

3 For each situation, identify an alternative behavior that would move you closer to your desired outcome for that situation.

Now that you've learned some great techniques for managing your emotions, let's move on to strengthening impulse control.

Takeaways

- Emotion regulation means identifying your feelings and consciously controlling the intensity of those feelings.
- Awareness of the emotion you are feeling allows you to make choices about how to respond.
- Emotions are transient and will fade in intensity if you just sit and experience them.
- The mind and body are inextricably linked and affect each other directly, so it's very important to tend to your physical needs, like sleep, diet, and exercise.
- Building emotional resilience will help you weather strong emotions and negative situations.
- Using the 3x3 Method can calm you quickly in a stressful or overwhelming moment.
- Identifying alternative behaviors allows you to respond to uncertainty in a way that promotes better outcomes.

<u>6</u> Improve Your Impulse Control

Overview

When we come into the world, we are very impulsive. Babies are impulsive and reactive, always seeking immediate gratification. When baby wants to eat, she tugs on Mom's shirt, looking for milk. When baby is curious about your nose, he reaches out and sticks his finger in your nostril. When baby needs to relieve herself, she goes right where she is, even if it's on your new couch. As frustrating as this can be, we expect this type of behavior from a baby, and we act accordingly.

As our brains develop, so do the brakes—our ability to control our impulses. Adults still need to relieve themselves, but we are able to wait for the restroom.

But as we will see in this chapter, competing needs, stimuli, and feelings can make impulse control challenging, especially for adults with ADHD. The ability to pause, evaluate a situation, and act appropriately requires executive functions, those core mental skills we've been talking about throughout this book. In the ADHD brain, executive functions are compromised, especially in stimulating or challenging settings.

Have you ever been impulsive? Most people with ADHD have struggled to control their impulses. On the ADHD blogs and in many ADHD books, you will often read about people engaging in sensational behaviors like gambling, sex, and excessive spending. The reality for most adults with ADHD is less exciting. You probably struggle with impulsivity in your daily life. Maybe you have trouble waiting before sending off a hasty e-mail response, you blurt things out in conversations, or you have trouble controlling how many sweets you eat. These are the areas where impulsivity can feel impossible to control. Human beings are pretty good at managing big life events like divorce, job loss, and death. But it's the everyday hassles like spilling your coffee, hitting every red light, or getting a paper cut that wear people down. The same factors are true for people with ADHD. Big acts of impulsivity like gambling or large purchases tend to be overcome. Things like speaking out of turn at work, speeding to beat a red light, or eating the last dessert are the impulsive behaviors that prevent life from running smoothly.

Developing adequate impulse control across all areas of life will help you live each day with more consistency, which will improve your quality of life, your success at work, and your relationships.

What *Not* to Do

I live in the heart of a major city and have two small children. Needless to say, sometimes my life is a noisy and chaotic ride. Just like most parents, I've noticed that "no" is my most frequently used word, especially in the evening when my kids are tired and their ability to control their behavior is compromised. Unfortunately, saying no is not very effective. Learning not to do something is generally harder than learning to do something. A big reason for this is that when we display a particular behavior or learn a new skill, there's some sort of reward at the end. For adults, the reward might be a sense of satisfaction, a raise at work, or praise from someone we care about. But when we don't do something, there is often no reward.

In this section, we will see that there *are* rewards for using inhibition to control impulses—they just take a little more effort to identify, especially in the moment.

This thought exercise will make things clear. Imagine for a moment that you are calmly reading a book on a park bench, and I walk up and ask you to blurt out something offensive to a stranger. You will probably look at me like I'm crazy, and you certainly won't say anything to the stranger. Why not? It's simple. In a calm mind-set, you are able to quickly realize that there could be negative consequences to suddenly shouting something offensive at a stranger.

So what's the reward? If you don't say something offensive to the stranger, the reward might be getting to sit peacefully and read your book, stay relaxed, or feel good about exercising self-control.

Now imagine that we do the whole thing over again, but this time I tell you the stranger just smashed your car door while parking and is about to walk off without telling you. You might be quick to jump up impulsively and say something offensive. In this second example, you are likely being hijacked by intense emotions, which makes it harder to control yourself. Or you might expect to be rewarded by getting the person's insurance information, which could save you lots of money in repairs.

The above example shows us some very important factors that contribute to impulse control that have nothing to do with ADHD. In order to control behaviors, you must quickly pause; assess possible outcomes, consequences, and rewards; and then act accordingly. ADHD makes it hard to take a pause and hard to put the brakes on impulsive behavior.

Let's do a couple of exercises that will help you learn to evaluate your actions and outcomes, and be more open to alternative options.

EXERCISE LINKING ACTION AND OUTCOME

Most people find the following exercise challenging. It requires you to look exclusively at your part in particular interactions and situations. It's easy to rationalize our behavior by explaining what the other person did or by saying the situation was unfair. It's harder to focus on your behavior and the actual outcome. By looking at only your role and behavior, you can begin to link actions and outcomes.

1 Think back to three recent examples of when you did something that had a negative consequence. Maybe you cursed in a meeting, blew off an appointment, overspent, or embarrassed yourself.

2 For each example, write down in your notebook the outcome or response to your behavior. For example: If you blurted out your opinion at the wrong time, what was the negative consequence? If you overspent, what was the negative effect on your finances or relationship?

3 For each example, write down the way you felt about the outcome. Remember, this is just about you, not about any other people who were involved. Instead of writing down something like, "I felt cheated, because if my coworker hadn't opened his big mouth, the boss would have invited me to the game instead of him," just write how you felt about the outcome. In the baseball game example, you might have felt sad, disappointed, left out, or embarrassed.

tip **Play the tape forward.** Before you act on an impulse, think about how things will play out. Envision what the outcome will be and how you will feel as a result. Hindsight is always 20/20—now it's time to get your foresight up to 20/20.

EXERCISE WHAT ARE YOUR OPTIONS?

One of the things I specialize in is helping people solve problems. Most situations have many more options than people initially realize. In this exercise, you will practice thinking of alternative options to respond in situations that didn't go well.

1 In your notebook, list the three examples you used from the previous exercise, "Linking Action and Outcome" (page 118).

2 For each example, list at least five behaviors you could have chosen instead. If you get stuck, get creative. If one option involves calling aliens to come help you, so be it. The point is to free yourself up and be mentally flexible.

3 For each example, choose one of the alternative behaviors that would have led to a more positive outcome. Write down the positive outcome that the alternative behavior would have led to.

tip **Pause and turn over stones.** When you are presented with a challenging situation and feel the pull to act impulsively, pause. Use this brief pause to think of a few alternative paths that might lead to a positive outcome. Leave no stone unturned.

More Thinking about Thinking

Back in chapter 4, we discussed metacognition, or thinking about thinking. I asked you to spend time developing your mental skills around observing what you are thinking. In this section, we will take metacognition further by applying it to behaviors in addition to thoughts. Before every behavior, there is a thought and a feeling. The pattern is the same for everyone: thought → feeling → behavior. So when you hear someone say, "Think before you act," or, "You're acting without thinking," you will know they are wrong at a basic level. Unfortunately, you are not off the hook, because they are correct at a higher level—the level of metacognition.

Here is an example: Kari walks into the living room to find that her boyfriend's coffee has been spilled onto her laptop. She blurts out, "Jamir, you idiot, what the heck is your problem? You don't care about my stuff!" Jamir, having no idea what she's talking about, fires back with his own negative statement. In short order, they are having an argument. After arguing for several minutes, Kari's kitten, Muffin Sweetie Cakes, emerges from under the table with coffee on her paws and mouth. In an instant, Kari and Jamir realize the kitten knocked over the coffee cup. They both begin to laugh.

The pattern that played out for Kari started with a thought: "Oh no, Jamir spilled coffee on my laptop." Then she had a feeling of anger. Finally, it became the behavior of shouting at him. She never paused to think about other possible causes, nor did she pause to think about her thinking and alternative ways to respond to the situation.

BREAKING THE REACTIVITY CYCLE

There are times in life when reacting quickly is of utmost importance. These situations are typically when survival or safety are at risk. The human brain is incredibly good at recognizing tiny changes in situations, and it can switch into a "flow state" where decision-making and behavior become seamless, leading to an exponential improvement in performance that can save a life. Unfortunately, this state is only temporary, and it has nothing to do with everyday reactions to frustrating events. Impulsively sending a nasty e-mail doesn't meet the criteria for safety and survival.

When you are being highly reactive, you are not being responsive. Impulsive reactions tend to lead to more trouble.

On the other hand, mindful responses tend to lead to less trouble and improved outcomes. So, how do you tap into this elusive mindful response and avoid the all-too-familiar impulsive reaction? It all starts with a pause, followed by a breath, then thoughts, and finally an action.

Impulsive Reaction

Stage 1 You are called an inappropriate name by a frustrated coworker.

Stage 2 You immediately send an e-mail to the whole company lambasting your coworker and telling all their dirty secrets.

Outcome You get fired.

Adaptive Response

Stage 1 You are called an inappropriate name by a frustrated coworker.

Stage 2 You pause.

Stage 3 You take a deep breath.

Stage 4 You evaluate your options.

Stage 5 You send an e-mail to your coworker asking for a meeting to discuss the incident.

Outcome Your relationship with the coworker improves, and your boss sees you as a possible future leader at the company.

The differences are obvious. In the reactive example, things happen quickly and have a very bad outcome. In the responsive example, things slow down, and the outcome is very positive.

Reactive

Stimulus ➡ Action ➡ Outcome

Responsive

Stimulus ➡ Pause ➡ Breath ➡ Evaluation ➡ Action ➡ Outcome

EXERCISE DEFUSION

ACT (short for Acceptance and Commitment Therapy) is a structured way of relating to our thoughts and behaviors. As a therapeutic approach, it has a lot of research and evidence behind it. Although there's an incredible wealth of helpful techniques in ACT, I want us to focus on practicing two simple steps to help you learn what's called *defusion*. Defusion is a way to decrease the intensity of thoughts and behaviors by separating your thoughts from your behaviors. If you have been following along since the beginning of this book, you know that awareness is the key to all change. In this exercise, you will use defusion to build awareness in order to improve your ability to respond with awareness.

1 In your notebook, write down what you are thinking and how you are feeling right now.

2 Example: "I have so much to do before work tomorrow. I'm feeling worried and inadequate."

3 Rewrite what you are thinking and feeling as though you were someone else observing you. Start your sentence with, "I've noticed . . ." or "I'm observing . . ."

EXAMPLE *"I've noticed that I'm feeling worried and inadequate, because I'm thinking about the many things I need to do before work tomorrow." Or, you might write it as, "I'm observing that I'm having a lot of thoughts about the things I need to do before work tomorrow, and it's making me feel worried and inadequate."*

4 Practice! Tomorrow, try to use this method of observing and labeling your thoughts and feelings at least twice.

5 After you practice tomorrow, write down what you observed about practicing the technique. "I've observed that practicing . . ."

tip **Remember to zoom out.** Just like a camera, you have the ability to zoom in and see your situation up close, but that may prevent you from seeing the whole picture. Zooming out is another way of taking a step back and noticing everything you are experiencing.

STOP SIGNS (STOP, THINK, OBSERVE, PLAN)

STOP is much like the 3x3 Method I presented in chapter 5. STOP (Stop, Think, Observe, Plan) is a way to ground yourself in the current moment, take inventory of your resources and the environment, and then make a plan for taking action.

STOP is widely used in outdoor survival training. You might be asking yourself, "Why is Phil bringing up outdoor survival? What's next, some sort of crazy mountain-climbing exercise?" but I'm sharing this technique with you because it's designed to help people get their mind under control and take responsive actions instead of reactive ones. It doesn't really matter if you are in the family room, the boardroom, or a cave in the wilderness—when you are mentally and emotionally hijacked, you will be impulsive and make poor choices.

When you use STOP, you increase your options and your ability to act on those options. The next time you find yourself in a tough interaction at home or work, try STOP.

Let's look at an example:

Kenyon just got to work late and noticed that everyone is in a big training meeting in the cafeteria. He sees his boss sitting by the door to the cafeteria. He automatically turns around and starts to head back to the parking lot to leave. At this point, he remembers to use STOP. He stops. He sits down on a bench to collect himself and slow his breathing down. Next, he thinks about what he is feeling and realizes that if he leaves, he will likely be punished for not showing up to work. Now he is observing his environment and the whole situation. While observing, he notices a schedule on the door of the cafeteria that says there will be a break in five minutes. Finally, he makes a plan. He plans to wait for the break so his entrance won't be so awkward, and then he will sign in and apologize for being late to the training.

If Kenyon had let his thoughts and feelings lead him down an impulsive path, he might have lost his job. Instead, he plans to act with integrity and honesty. He will keep his job and feel better about himself.

tip **When all else fails, just stop.** Even if you can't remember all the steps in STOP, the defusion techniques of observing and labeling, or the 3x3 Method, you can simply stop and take a pause. A pause, even if just for a moment, will always decrease your impulsivity.

PRACTICING SOCIAL OBSERVATION

Sometimes the best option is to use cues from other people to figure out the best way to behave. Granted, there are times when you need to blaze your own trail, but those are usually deliberate choices, not reactions based in impulsivity. If you feel like cracking a joke and everyone else is quiet and sad, impulsivity might be getting the best of you. Taking cues from other people in the environment is a common human behavior, and it can save you from making a misjudgment about how to behave.

1 Go to a public place like a shopping mall, college campus, or food court—any place where you can observe groups of people interacting.

2 Observe a minimum of two or three groups, one at a time. As you observe a group, look at their facial expressions and how they are talking and moving.

3 Based on your observations, try to make up a story about what they might be talking about or where they just came from and where they are going.

4 Without actually joining or interrupting any groups (don't be impulsive), decide how you should act if you were to approach the group. How loudly should you speak? Should you be funny or serious? Would it make sense to walk fast or slow as you approach them?

(tip) **Check your thoughts against what you see.** Let's say you remember a funny joke and want to tell it to your friend. First look at the environment and see what others are doing. Would it make sense to tell a joke in this environment? Is it the right timing? This is a great way to double-check your social awareness.

Delay of Gratification

What does it mean to delay gratification? In simple terms, it means waiting for a period of time before obtaining a reward. For example, "I'm going to eat my ice cream right now," becomes, "I'm going to wait until after dinner to eat my ice cream." It might look simple in this example, but it can become much more complex if the immediate reward is buying a new car or financing your first home.

The ability to delay gratification is deeply rooted in core mental skills. It takes a good amount of mental resources to mindfully evaluate all the factors that shape your decision to "buy now" or "buy later." In some ways, delaying gratification is one of the most important of your core skills. This is because the act of delaying gratification requires the use of several major mental skills at the same time. You must manage emotions, accurately recall memories, keep impulsivity in check, plan ahead, and remain mentally flexible in order to choose to receive a reward later.

There is a *huge* bit of good news here: The more often you delay gratification, the better you become at using a host of core skills. Plus, you'll get a boost in self-confidence after repeated successful attempts.

The most important research in the delay of gratification took place at Stanford University. You might have heard of the "marshmallow study" done in the 1960s by professor Walter Mischel. In brief, four- and five-year-olds were offered one marshmallow to eat now or two marshmallows if they waited for 15 minutes without eating the single marshmallow. I don't know about you, but I would struggle with that, and I'm in my 40s! You might be thinking, "Great, I would struggle, too. Why should I care about this study?" Well, over the next 40 years, the researchers checked on most of the children and found that the kids who were able to wait (delay gratification) did better in school and work, had better relationships, had better health—the benefits went on and on. Maybe you're still on the fence, thinking, "I'm not a child! Who cares?" Well, *you* should care, because your ability to delay gratification has a direct impact on your bank account, waistline, relationships, job performance, and even parenting.

But in my opinion, the most relevant research for adults with ADHD comes from Robert Sapolsky, also of Stanford. Sapolsky calls this phenomenon "The Dopamine Jackpot," and it's typically an *aha!* moment for my clients. He found that the rush of dopamine, the neurochemical that allows us to feel reward, is released a short time *before* the reward is actually achieved. This is why the last 5 to 10 percent of a project's completion is the hardest—because the reward has already happened inside your brain!

SHORT- VERSUS LONG-TERM THINKING

Imagine this: You're on your way to work, running late. You approach an intersection with a stoplight, the light turns yellow, and you are still a ways from the intersection. You feel stressed and impulsive, and you face a choice. Your short-term thoughts might be, "Step on the gas. I've got to make this light!" Short-term thinking in this situation could get you or someone else hurt. Risking running a red light is a bad choice, period. But you are in a short-term mind-set, and the gratification of making it through the intersection is all that matters in the moment. If you were to exercise long-term thinking, your thoughts might be, "Do I try to make the light? It looks dangerous, and being another couple of minutes late is better than risking serious injury or another traffic ticket." In this example, you can see the difference between short-term and long-term thinking.

Short- versus long-term thinking is at play in nearly every situation. Granted, there are actual life-and-death situations, when survival mechanisms take over and there seems to be very little or no thinking happening, just action. That said, most situations, like deciding to eat dessert after dinner or choosing to hold off on another frivolous purchase, do use a balance of short- and long-term thinking. Earlier in this chapter, we saw how important it is to evaluate your options in order to avoid impulsivity. Evaluating the short-term and long-term effects of a choice is equally important. Impulsivity lives in the short term. Impulsivity is like a teenager—everything is about today, never tomorrow.

EXERCISE **WHAT ARE THE CONSEQUENCES?**

1 For each example below, write down in your notebook the possible effects your choice would have in your life. Make sure to write down the short-, medium-, and long-term consequences.

2 Once you have listed all the possible consequences, choose which set of consequences you would want in that situation. Write down your decision with a short explanation of why you made it.

3 After you've done all the examples, reflect on your experience. Was it hard or easy? Did you feel pulled to think in the short term or the long term?

EXAMPLE 1 *Out of the blue, you are presented with an offer from the owner of a competing company. The offer is to double your salary if you come work for that company, but you must quit your current job before they will officially hire you. Will you take the offer?*

EXAMPLE 2 *You need to be up early tomorrow for a big day—you'll be showing out-of-town friends around your town. It's already one hour past your optimal bedtime when you see an online ad that says there's a free sneak preview of a new blockbuster movie available online before midnight. Do you watch it?*

EXAMPLE 3 *One day, in front of the grocery store, you meet a nice family that's giving away puppies, kittens, and baby rabbits. They offer you the option to adopt one of the cute little pets for free and take it home. What will you decide?*

(tip) Think about what someone else would say. Before you make an impulsive decision to receive an immediate reward, think of two people you respect, and ask yourself what they would advise you to do.

Takeaways

- Impulse control is easier when you are in a calm state of mind in which you can pause, evaluate, and decide how to act.
- Behind every behavior is a pattern of "thought, feeling, behavior."
- It's better to be responsive than reactive.
- Reactive: Stimulus → Action → Outcome
- Responsive: Stimulus → Pause → Breath → Evaluation → Action → Outcome
- Defusion is a way to separate thoughts from behaviors.
- Using STOP (Stop, Think, Observe, Plan) decreases impulsivity.
- You can observe other people to get clues for how to behave in a certain situation.
- The ability to delay gratification has a direct positive impact on your finances, health, relationships, career, and even parenting.

7 Live Your Best Life with ADHD

Congratulations!

You did it! You are awesome! It's an incredible accomplishment to have completed this book. Seriously, pat yourself on the back. Take a moment to notice how you feel. Let your positive voice speak loudly to you. You now have the skills to harness your core executive functions in order to work smarter and be more productive, less stressed, and more in control of your life.

I have guided you through information and practical techniques that you can sustain over several decades. However, as with learning a new language, you need to use your new skills regularly in order to get the full benefit. There's no reason not to. At the end of this rainbow is a pot full of self-confidence. Continue to grow your confidence, not only by using the skills in this book but also by referring back to it. This book is a resource that will always be here for you to lean on. If you find your ADHD symptoms bubbling up or your self-confidence going down, just grab your notebook and reflect on the incredible knowledge you've amassed.

Think about it. Now you know how to make hard decisions. Now you know how to organize your projects and get them done. Now you have the skills to help you regulate tough emotions. Now you understand how to manage your time. Now you no longer need to be afraid of complex instructions or a daunting task. Now you know how to make lasting memories. Now you have techniques for keeping distractions at arm's length. Now you can lock into sustained attention and focus. Now you are able to see multiple perspectives to solve problems. Now you can shift mental gears with more flexibility. Now you are more aware of your own thoughts and feelings and can't be pushed around by negativity. Now you have the ability to make life more manageable and keep overwhelm in check. It's truly incredible. Go you!

Making Friends with Your ADHD

Now that you're familiar with your individual ADHD style and your strengths and weaknesses, you will be able to create plans for success every time you meet a new challenge. Whether the challenge is a big project at work, a novel situation at home, a new emotional struggle, or any other way that your ADHD is tripping you up, you are prepared to meet it. Your newfound ability to use powerful tools and techniques to mindfully plan for action around challenges will set you apart from the pack.

Researching and writing this book reminded me of the many options that are available in any situation. The saying, "You get what you get, and you don't get upset," no longer applies to you. You now have the unique ability to change the course of your life by managing your ADHD in very effective ways. The reality is that most adults with ADHD don't take the steps you have taken. Most people either try to tough it out or just take a prescription medication without any additional skills training.

Don't forget that the skills you have will be helpful to those who are close to you. You can guide others, with or without ADHD, through their challenges. When you help others, you will be helping yourself by deepening your learning and use of your skills. You now have wisdom. Share it.

The following exercises will help you remember how to work smarter over the long haul.

EXERCISE WHAT WERE YOUR FAVORITE TECHNIQUES AND WHY?

1 Turn to a blank page in your notebook and create a list of all the techniques you can remember without looking back in the book.

2 Go back and scan the chapters and your notes. Add the techniques and insights you found helpful and forgot to list.

3 Decide on about 10 of the most useful techniques you encountered. Once you have this shorter list, write one or two sentences about why each one is important to you.

By following the above steps, you will improve your knowledge retention and the "stickiness" of your new skills.

EXERCISE CREATE A ONE-WEEK STRATEGIES PLAN

You can create this plan in your calendar, in a spreadsheet, or even just on a piece of paper. You can change it as needed, but if you change it, remember to do so with mindful intention, determination, and purpose. No more flying by the seat of your pants in a state of chaos.

1 In your chosen format (calendar, spreadsheet, notebook, paper), create a weekly plan that will serve as a template for each week in the near future.

2 Decide when you will sleep, exercise, and eat, and write it down.

3 Decide what times of day you will do specific types of tasks, based on your particular energy, focus, and life demands, and write it down. Map it all out. This will serve as a foundation that will quickly get you into a groove.

THERAPY, MEDICATION, AND OTHER SUPPORTS

You have learned many valuable strategies on your journey through this book. However, you may still want some additional tools and information. Here are a few more supports.

Medication. Many people who have been accurately diagnosed with ADHD pursue stimulant medications. When used correctly, medications can be very helpful. However, there's not a "one size fits all" medication. It's important to seek treatment from a specialist who understands the nuances of ADHD medications.

Cognitive Behavioral Therapy (CBT). CBT is an extremely valuable tool for managing adult ADHD. There is considerable research behind CBT showing its effectiveness with ADHD, as well as anxiety and depression.

Skills Training. Equipping yourself with an assortment of skills is good in any situation. Adults with ADHD can improve their functioning and quality of life by learning more skills. Both the Beyond Focused and Totally ADD websites are great resources, offering video-based skills training.

Support Groups. There are great support groups and organizations out there for people with ADHD. There's no reason to go it alone. The best sources for ADHD support groups are Children and Adults with ADHD (CHADD) (chadd.org) and the Attention Deficit Disorder Association (ADDA) (add.org).

Staying on Track:
Tune-Ups and Check-Ins

During my final meeting with clients, I often tell them that people are a lot like cars or other machines. People need tune-ups to continue running well. It's easy and normal to fall out of habit with a new skill. I let people know to expect a dip in effectiveness after a few weeks—again, that is totally normal. However, this time around, it will be different. Instead of falling out of routine or practice and saying to yourself, "I knew it! I can't keep anything going; I can't change," I want you to simply label it from the standpoint of an observer: "Ahh, I've slipped on my routine. Phil said this could happen, and this is normal. What do I need to do to get back in the game?" If you want to nearly ensure that this type of thing won't sneak up on you, do regular check-ins with yourself. On a weekly basis, ask yourself what's going well and what's not going well, and create a plan to improve where needed. Slipups and fall-backs are not the problem; it's what you do when you are faced with them. If you slip, stumble, or fall, get back up and move forward!

POST-TEST: SELF-ASSESSMENT

A great way to check in with yourself on an ongoing basis is to use the self-assessments from chapter 1. By retaking those assessment quizzes on a monthly basis and keeping track of your answers for comparison, you can easily monitor your improvements and any backsliding that has taken place.

Give it a try now. Go back and retake the self-assessments for Attention and Focus (page 6), Organizing and Planning (page 7), Mental Flexibility (page 8), Emotion Regulation (page 9), and Impulse Control (page 10). Has anything changed? Where have you made progress already? Do you need to increase your efforts in any areas?

MAINTAIN YOUR MOMENTUM

In order to maintain your momentum, it's critical that you schedule two types of check-ins. The first is the brief weekly check-in I suggested, and the second is the monthly self-assessment.

The weekly check-in needs to happen at the same time, on the same day, each week. By having a predictable time to check in, you will greatly increase the likelihood that it gets done. Try to do the weekly check-ins every week. Week after week, you will be keeping your progress going.

The monthly self-assessment should also be done at a consistent and predictable time. An easy way to do it is to place it on a *day* of the month, not a date each month. For example, rather than having to schedule continued self-assessments for a specific date near the beginning or end of each month, you can choose a day, such as the first Friday of each month or the last Monday of each month. You won't need to do the follow-up assessments forever, just for a few months to get things in place. After you have done the self-assessments every month for about four months, you can do them a couple of times a year or as needed.

I hope you can now see just how incredible the future will be for you. The thorns in your side and the weights that have held you down are nearly gone. As you continue to get better, become stronger, and allow your self-confidence to blossom, your life will grow in wonderful ways. Don't wait! Stand up, put one foot in front of the other, and walk with your head held high. You are going to accomplish great things. Your future is waiting. Go get it.

Resources

APPS, WEBSITE BLOCKERS, TO-DO LIST BUILDERS

Blacklist, website blocker by Masterbuilders: https://appadvice.com/app/blacklist-website-blocker/1081580076

Beyond Focused, the author's site, offering video programs for adult ADHD: www.beyondfocused.com

CreativeLive, "Get into Your Creative Flow," online class by Steven Kotler: https://www.creativelive.com/class/get-into-your-creative-flow-steven-kotler

Alex Cruz Music: https://www.alexcruzmusic.com

Due, a reminder and task-capture app: www.dueapp.com

FocusMe, a website and app-blocking app: https://focusme.com

Happify, a thought and mind-set app: https://happify.com

Pacifica, a stress management app: www.thinkpacifica.com

Remember the Milk, a to-do list app: www.rememberthe milk.com

SelfControl, a website and app-blocking app: https://self controlapp.com

StayFocusd, a website and app-blocking app: https://chrome.google.com/webstore/detail/stayfocusd/laankejkbhbdhmipf mgcngdelahlfoji

Tile, a tool and app for finding lost items: www.thetileapp.com

MORE READING

I recommend taking a look at the books I've listed here. In some cases, I have seen these books literally change lives.

ADHD BOOKS

The ADHD Advantage: What You Thought Was a Diagnosis May Be Your Greatest Strength by Dale Archer, MD
Dale is a psychiatrist specializing in the treatment of ADHD. His book takes a novel approach to adult ADHD. He helps people identify how their ADHD can be an asset in their lives rather than a deficit.

The ADHD Effect on Marriage: Understand and Rebuild Your Relationship in Six Steps by Melissa Orlov
Melissa is an award-winning author and Harvard scholar. Her book provides sound advice for managing ADHD within relationships.

ADHD: What Everyone Needs to Know by Stephen P. Hinshaw and Katherine Ellison
Stephen is a professor of psychology who serves on the executive committee of the Institute of Human Development at UC Berkeley, where he researches ADHD. Katherine is a Pulitzer Prize–winning journalist with extensive knowledge of ADHD. Their book provides a highly accurate breakdown of everything you have ever wondered about ADHD.

The Mindfulness Prescription for Adult ADHD: An 8-Step Program for Strengthening Attention, Managing Emotions, and Achieving Your Goals by Lidia Zylowska, MD
Lidia is a psychiatrist who cofounded the UCLA Mindful Awareness Research Center, where she conducted cutting-edge research into the use of mindfulness in the management of ADHD. Her book is chock-full of everything you

need to know in order to harness mindfulness and manage your ADHD.

Scattered: How Attention Deficit Disorder Originates and What You Can Do about It by Gabor Maté, MD

Gabor is a physician and an internationally best-selling author. His book sheds light on a rarely discussed and sometimes controversial connection between childhood attachment theory and ADHD.

GENERAL HEALTH AND PSYCHOLOGY BOOKS

Design for Strengths: Applying Design Thinking to Individual and Team Strengths by John K. Coyle

John is an Olympic medalist speed skater and sought-after keynote speaker with deep expertise in using theories pioneered at Stanford for designing experiences. His book provides you with a framework to harness your strengths and cut bait on your weaknesses.

Go Wild: Free Your Body and Mind from the Afflictions of Civilization by John J. Ratey, MD, and Richard Manning

John is the only person to make it on this list twice! He is associate clinical professor of psychiatry at Harvard Medical School and an expert on ADHD. In this book, he and Richard Manning provide an overview and in-depth information about how food can either help or hurt us.

Never Split the Difference: Negotiate as If Your Life Depends on It by Chris Voss with Tahl Raz

Chris is the former lead hostage negotiator for the FBI. His book, an unlikely choice for this list, provides much more than information about negotiation. It teaches skills that can help anyone communicate more effectively in all aspects of life.

Spark: The Revolutionary New Science of Exercise and the Brain by John J. Ratey, MD, with Eric Hagerman

As an associate clinical professor of psychiatry at Harvard Medical School and an expert on ADHD, John provides in this book incredibly useful information about how exercise can be used to strengthen and heal the brain.

The Rise of Superman: Decoding the Science of Ultimate Human Performance by Steven Kotler

Steven is a best-selling author and the director of research at the Flow Genome Project. His book is an incredibly engaging account of how extreme athletes use extreme states of focus called FLOW to reach superhuman performance.

References

Biederman, Joseph, Timothy Wilens, Eric Mick, Stephen V. Faraone, Wendy Weber, Shannon Curtis, Ayanna Thornell, Kiffany Pfister, Jennifer Garcia Jetton, and Jennifer Soriano. "Is ADHD a Risk Factor for Psychoactive Substance Use Disorders? Findings from a Four-Year Prospective Follow-up Study." *Journal of the American Academy of Child and Adolescent Psychiatry* 36, no. 1 (January 1997): 21–29. doi:10.1097/00004583-199701000-00013.

Boissiere, Phil. "30 Seconds to Mindfulness," 3x3 Method. TEDxNaperville. Accessed September 24, 2018. https://www .youtube.com/watch?v=ad7HqXEc2Sc&feature=youtu.be.

Colebrooke, Lawrence. *Special Operations Mental Toughness: The Invincible Mindset of Delta Force Operators, Navy Seals, Army Rangers, and Other Elite Warriors!* CreateSpace Independent Publishing Platform, 2015.

Ferriss, Timothy. *The 4-Hour Workweek: Escape 9–5, Live Anywhere, and Join the New Rich.* New York: Crown Publishers, 2009.

Fuchs, Eberhard, and Gabriele Flügge. "Adult Neuroplasticity: More than 40 Years of Research." *Neural Plasticity.* 2014 (May 4, 2014). doi:10.1155/2014/541870. https://www.hindawi .com/journals/np/2014/541870/.

Harvard Health Publishing. "Why Nutritionists Are Crazy about Nuts: Mounting Evidence Suggests That Eating Nuts and Seeds Daily Can Lower Your Risk of Diabetes and Heart

Disease and May Even Lengthen Your Life." *Harvard Women's Health Watch.* June 2017. https://www.health.harvard.edu /nutrition/why-nutritionists-are-crazy-about-nuts.

Haynes, Trevor. "Dopamine, Smartphones, and You: A Battle for Your Time." Harvard University Science in the News Blog. May 1, 2018. http://sitn.hms.harvard.edu/flash/2018 /dopamine-smartphones-battle-time/.

Kessler, Ronald C., Lenard Adler, Minnie Ames, Olga Demler, Steve Faraone, Eva Hiripi, Mary J. Howes, Robert Jin, Kristin Asecnik, Thomas Spencer, T. Bedirhanustun, and Ellen E. Walters. "The World Health Organization Adult ADHD Self-Report Scale (ASRS): A Short Screening Scale for Use in the General Population." *Psychological Medicine* 35 (2005): 245–56. doi:10.1017/S0033291704002892.

Kotler, Steven. Conversation with author. See also "Get into Your Creative Flow." Online class at CreativeLive. Accessed September 25, 2018. https://www.creativelive.com/class /get-into-your-creative-flow-steven-kotler.

MacLeod, Colin M. "Half a Century of Research on the Stroop Effect: An Integrative Review." *Psychological Bulletin* 109, no. 2 (March 1991): 163–203.

Mischel, W., E. B. Ebbesen, and A. Raskoff Zeiss. "Cognitive and Attentional Mechanisms in Delay of Gratification." *Journal of Personality and Social Psychology* 21, no. 2 (February 1972), 204-18.

Ratey, John J. with Eric Hagerman. *Spark: The Revolutionary New Science of Exercise and the Brain.* New York: Little, Brown and Company, 2008.

Sapolsky, Robert. "Dopamine Jackpot! Sapolsky on the Science of Pleasure." FORA.tv. February 15, 2011. https://www.youtube.com/watch?v=axrywDP9Ii0.

Sullivan, Meg. "Trouble in Paradise: UCLA Book Enumerates Challenges Faced by Middle-Class L.A. Families." *Health + Behavior*. June 19, 2012. http://newsroom.ucla.edu/releases/trouble-in-paradise-new-ucla-book.

Index

A

Acceptance and Commitment
Therapy (ACT), 122–123
Addiction, 57–58
ADHD. *See* Attention Deficit
Hyperactivity Disorder
(ADHD)
Archer, Dale, 32
Attentional shifting, 85–87
Attention and focus. *See also*
Memory
assessment quiz, 6
attentional shifting, 85–87
managing distractions, 32–36
overview, 16–17, 43
and project planning, 39–43
remembering and following
instructions, 27–31
sustaining, 36–39
symptom management, 12–13
Attention Deficit Hyperactivity
Disorder (ADHD)
and intelligence, 4
management strategies,
133–134, 136–137
supports for, 135
symptoms, xii–xiii
talking with coworkers
about, 63–64
talking with family and friends
about, 107–109
Avoidance, 50–52

B

Backup planning, 77–79
Breaks, taking, 38
Breathing, 25, 34, 98, 105–106

C

Cannibal Task, 60
Clutter, 46–49
Cognitive Behavioral Therapy
(CBT), 135
Cognitive flexibility (CF)
assessment quiz, 8
backup planning, 77–79
metacognition, 79–83
overview, 67–70, 89
perspective taking, 74–77, 79
problem-solving, 70–73
transitions, 83–88
Cognitive skills, 11. *See also*
Core skills
Consequences, 128–129
Core skills
assessment, 5–10
overview, ix–x, 2–5
strengthening, 11–14
Coyle, John K., 72

D

Defusion, 122–123
Digital devices, 33, 57–60
Distractions, 32–36
Dopamine, 3, 57–58, 127
"Dopamine Jackpot," 127

E

Emotion regulation
  assessment quiz, 9
  identifying emotions, 93–98
  managing negative
    emotions, 105–107
  managing
    overwhelm, 109–112
  mind-body
    connection, 98–101
  overview, 91–92, 113
  resilience, 101–104
Emotions, 23, 26, 33, 45, 82–83,
  88. *See also* Emotion
  regulation
Empathy, 75
Evolution, 23–24, 33
Excitement, 95
Executive functions, ix–xi.
  See also Core skills
Exercise, 18–19, 100–101

F

Feelings, 93–94. *See also*
  Emotion regulation;
  Emotions
Ferriss, Timothy, 104
Focus. *See* Attention and focus
Forgetfulness, 16, 18.
  See also Memory

G

Goal-setting, 54
Gratification, delaying, 126–129

I

Impulse control
  assessment quiz, 10
  delaying
    gratification, 126–129
  evaluating actions and
    outcomes, 116–119
  overview, 115–116, 130
  reactivity cycle, 120–125

Instructions, remembering and
  following, 27–31
Internal distractions, 33
Interruptions, 58–59, 88

K

Kotler, Steven, 38

L

Lateral thinking, 70
Long-term thinking, 127–129

M

"Marshmallow study," 126–127
Medication, 135
Memory
  and following
    instructions, 27–31
  improving overall, 22–27
  overview, 16–17
  strengthening working, 17–21
Mental fatigue, 38
Mental flexibility. *See* Cognitive
  flexibility (CF)
Metacognition, 79–83, 119–125
Metaphors, 24, 26
Mind-body connection, 98–101
Mindful intention, 84–85
Mindfulness, 105–106
Mischel, Walter, 126–127
Mnemonics, 25, 27

N

Narratives, 20
Negative emotions, 23, 33, 45, 88,
  91–92, 94. *See also* Emotion
  regulation
  managing, 105–107
Neuroplasticity, 11–12
Neurotransmitters, 3
Norepinephrine, 3
Novelty-seeking, 36
Nutrition, 100–101

O

Organizing and planning
  assessment quiz, 7
  to-do lists, 61–63
  levels of organization, 46–49
  overview, 45–46, 65
  prioritization, 52–55
  task initiation, 50–52
  time management, 56–60
Overall memory, 22–27
Overwhelm, 109–112

P

Pausing, 59, 69, 75–77, 79, 81, 88, 107, 119
Perspective taking, 74–77, 79
PET (pause, evaluate, trust), 59
Pictographs, 23–24, 27
Planning. *See* Organizing and planning
Plasticity, 11–12
Positive emotions, 23, 95
Prefrontal cortex (PFC), x, 2–3, 92
Prioritization, 52–55
Problem-solving, 70–73
Procrastination, 45, 50–52
Project planning, 39–43, 48–49. *See also* Organizing and planning

R

Ratey, John, 101
Reactivity cycles, 120–125
Rehearsal, 25
Relationships
  coworkers, 63–64
  family and friends, 107–109
Resilience, 101–104
Rewards, 42, 116–117, 127

S

Sapolsky, Robert, 127
Schedules, 39
Self-monitoring, 82–83
Self-talk, 19, 63
Serotonin, 98
Shame, 94
Short-term thinking, 127–129
Skills training, 135
Sleep, 18–19, 99–101
Smartphones, 33, 57–60
Social observation, 125
STOP (Stop, Think, Observe, Plan), 123–124
Stress, 18, 33, 99
Support groups, 135

T

Task switching, 67–68. *See also* Cognitive flexibility (CF)
3x3 Method, 105–106
Time management, 56–60
Timers, 52
To-do lists, 61–63
Transitions, 83–88
Triaging, 53

U

Uncertainty, 109, 111–112

V

Virtuous cycles, 46

W

Working memory, 17–21
Workplace, 63–64, 87
Writing, and memory, 23–24

Y

"Yes," saying, 58–59

About the Author

Phil Boissiere, MFT, has spent the last decade treating adults with ADHD in the high-pressured environment of Silicon Valley. On top of his clinical training, Phil has pursued advanced training in the assessment and treatment of ADHD from Massachusetts General Hospital and Harvard University. Phil cofounded Silicon Valley's premiere adult ADHD clinic in partnership with two Stanford medical doctors. He also founded the online resource for adults with ADHD, Beyond Focused. As a clinical expert, Phil has been featured on major media outlets such as PBS, ABC News, *Good Morning America*, and others.